Marine Radio For Recreational Boaters

How to Sound Like a Pro on Your Marine VHF Radio

Scott Wilson

A Lubber's Guide

Copyright © 2020 by Lubber's Guides Press, Seattle, Washington.

No part of this publication may be reproduced, stored in a retrieval system, or transmitted in any form or by any means, electronic, mechanical, photocopying, recording, scanning, or otherwise, except as permitted under Section 107 or 108 of the 1976 United States Copyright Act, without the prior written permission of the publisher. Requests to the publisher for permission should be directed to info@forlubbers.com.

ISBN: 978-0-9977760-6-5

Limit of Liability/Disclaimer of Warranty: The publisher and the author make no representations or warranties with respect to the accuracy or completeness of the contents of this work and specifically disclaim all warranties, including without limitation warranties of fitness for a particular purpose. No warranty may be created or extended by sales or promotional materials. The advice and strategies contained herein may not be suitable for every situation. This work is sold with the understanding that the publisher is not engaged in rendering medical, legal, or other professional advice or services. If professional assistance is required, the services of a competent professional person should be sought. Neither the publisher nor the author shall be liable for damages arising herefrom. The fact that an individual, organization, or website is referred to in this work as a citation and/or potential source of further information does not mean that the author or the publisher endorses the information the individual, organization, or website may provide or recommendations they/it may make. Further, readers should be aware that websites listed in this work may have changed or disappeared between when this work was written and when it is read.

For Jack Binns, the first mariner in distress whose radio calls brought salvation to 739 souls the morning of January 23rd, 1909.

Table of Contents

Preface --- 1

Acknowledgments --- 3

Introduction -- 5

The Radio System   7

Common Equipment, Uncommon Understanding -------------------- 8

Why VHF Is Hard -- 12

Making VHF Radio Understandable -------------------------------- 16

Listening   20

Developing Listening Skills -- 21

Making Sense of Radio Language ----------------------------------- 27

Elements of a Radio Conversation ---------------------------------- 34

Following the Rules -- 39

Speaking   44

Fitting the Format to Your Need ------------------------------------ 45

Specialized Protocols -- 62

Emergency Protocols -- 67

Using Radio in the Real World -------------------------------------- 83

Advanced Radio Techniques --------------------------------------- 101

Advanced Radio Protocols --- 109

Common Radio Problems -- 117

Operation and Troubleshooting   124

Understanding Marine Radio Technology ------------------------ 125

Radio Installation -- 147

Preface

For whatever reason, talking on the radio comes easily to some people, but not others.

Maybe it's because I grew up chatting with friends by walkie-talkie or CB, or went through a series of jobs in my younger years that involved a lot of radio work, but it's always come pretty naturally to me. Not that I don't make bonehead mistakes or sound stupid on the air from time to time—everyone does—but I've always been comfortable picking up the mike and starting a conversation. And I like to think those conversations have been understandable, polite, and to the point more often than not... appropriate uses of the shared spectrum all mariners rely on.

It's often been equally clear that others around me have been less comfortable in that role. Or, and maybe worse, that they have felt a little *too* comfortable, while their disregard for the uses and capabilities of the medium have inconvenienced or even endangered others around them.

Since I'm no expert in the physics of radio, it was clear the difference between them and me wasn't a depth of technical knowledge. Instead, I believe it was a familiarity with patterns, with systems, and with the exposure to how the general community of radio users creates the expectations and rhythms of communication. Radio is a shared medium that requires common courtesy and adherence to protocol for it to function for everyone.

Yet the importance of understanding some of the most basic technical details of how marine radios work has also been driven home to me repeatedly over the years.

Before dawn on a cold, rainy spring morning in 2008, halfway up the Inside Passage in a narrow inlet about 30 miles north of Bella Bella, I woke up to the sensation of icy seawater lapping at my foot as it dangled over the edge of my berth. I'd run the boat aground the night before and was catnapping as I waited for the high tide to float her off again, but something had gone wrong—

she was flooding as the tide came in instead of floating.

I splashed across the cabin sole through the water to the VHF radio mounted at the companionway and tried to hail Prince Rupert Coast Guard. I'd been in touch with them the night before, letting them know my location and situation and setting up a comms schedule in case something went wrong. But the next scheduled check-in wasn't for a few hours, and things were going wrong *now*.

After several calls, there was still no reply.

With an icy ball in my gut, I realized that with the keel aground, the antenna at the top of the mast was canted over much lower than it had been the night before. It was no longer high enough for the signal to clear the dense, mist-faded firs lining the inlet. Nor did the radio have the power to punch through them; the house battery bank had been in use all night.

I reached down and flicked the battery selector over to "All" to combine the power from the house battery with that of the starter battery bank to provide more juice to the radio. Maybe, I thought, it would have enough power to punch through the trees.

Prince Rupert answered on the next call.

This wasn't a life-or-death episode, nor was it any great feat of computational physics and electrical theory… I just happened to know that VHF is a line-of-sight technology and that it is dependent on transmission power to overcome interference. So by putting two and two together, I realized that with my line-of-sight reduced because of the lower mast height, I needed more power to get through.

This book aims to give you just enough basic radio knowledge that you will be comfortable troubleshooting problems with a robust sense of how radio conversations are conducted in the real world, and the appropriate techniques to understand, and make yourself understood in, radio conversations.

Acknowledgments

This is a book that has been a long time in coming and one that I imagined was going to be a lot faster and easier to write than proved to be the case. I mean, it's not a great work of literature or anything, but what I thought was going to be about eight months of work and some messing about with commas turned into something more like two years and a great deal more correspondence, research, and vacillation than is typically the case for me.

For those reasons, I am far more indebted to various friends and associates than ever, and would like to spread around whatever credit is due, while, naturally, assuming sole responsibility myself for whatever deficits may remain in the material.

First, however, I will give myself some credit: when stuck on an early draft that was obviously not working, but without any obvious reasons why, I was smart enough to ship it off to my friend and fellow writer and sailor John Juliano first. He pinpointed not only where it was broken, but also proposed the solution that led—after considerable toil, sweat, and tears—to the final form you see here today. You may still dislike it, I don't know, but I do know you would have liked it a lot less without John's invaluable suggestions.

Later drafts ended up in the hands of other old salts: my stepfather, Scott Graebel, and friend Ed Frye. Both provided incisive, point-by-point feedback and offered kind words for the things that were working well and effective suggestions for other additions or corrections.

Their spouses, Linda Graebel (my mother) and Terry Moon (my other mother) offered encouragement, support, and quite a lot of food.

My friend, fellow nautical writer, and occasional dock mate Joshua Wheeler also provided valuable insights, comments, and suggestions at key points in the process.

Other reviewers along the way include such luminaries of Pacific Northwest nautical circles as Captain Dave Petrich, Christian Gruye, and Brion Toss, and their input and encouragement provided much motivation and energy where my enthusiasm sometimes flagged.

Though I ultimately wasn't able to use nearly as much of the material as I would have liked, I particularly want to thank Jack Binns' eldest granddaughter, Virginia Utermohlen Lovelace, for sending me an early copy of the first volume of his unpublished memoirs. Extensively annotated by Virginia herself, a writer and retired professor, "Dots and Dashes" offered not only firsthand testimony of the *Republic* incident—the first radio-coordinated rescue in maritime history—but invaluable perspective on the early development and use of marine wireless. Early drafts of this book had far more of Binnsy's story in them, as it is an enthralling one… unfortunately, I was reaching too hard for narrative in what is more properly an instructional book and had to leave most of it on the cutting room floor.

Finally, thanks to my editor, Chrissy Cutting, and cover designer and graphic artist, Yuka Highbridge, both of whom consistently turn in a far higher caliber of work than what they charge me for.

Introduction

This isn't like any other book about marine radio you have read.

Once upon a time, you needed one of those thick technical manuals to tell you how electromagnetic radiation was produced by feeding alternating current onto a conductor, where the oscillating electrons would set up propagating waves that could be received by another such conductor a few feet or miles away. Those technical details—which probably made your eyes glaze over just now—were important. Radios were primitive and had to be installed, configured, and operated by experts, or at least very well-educated amateurs.

But that's not the case today. Any lubber can unbox a VHF and plug it into an off-the-shelf antenna and reach out and touch someone twenty miles away. And let's be honest... you didn't even plug the antenna in yourself, did you?

But you're not just touching one person twenty miles away when you use it. You're touching everyone on that channel *within* twenty miles. And that makes it a lot more nerve-racking, doesn't it?

The hard part of marine radio today isn't radio theory. It's radio *practice*. What to say. When to speak. How to say it properly. How to interpret what you hear back. What to do if you don't hear *anything* back.

That's mostly what this book is about.

The operating theory behind this guide is that you don't need to know every last detail of how radios and electromagnetic waves work in order to use them. There are, of course, highly technical reasons why certain frequency bands are better for certain uses. Yet, most radio users do not need to understand how ground waves or sky waves or skip zones work to understand that one channel is good for reaching someone 40 miles away while another is better for reaching 400 miles.

The book doesn't get into any deep discussions on wavelengths, the ionosphere, or modulation techniques. There will be no pontification on the genius of Heinrich Hertz, and no mention of cycles or layers. It will deal with the practical effects of those physical phenomena as experienced by the average boater. It will only go into the technical details to the extent that it is is absolutely necessary to perform basic operations or troubleshooting. If you find a mathematical equation anywhere in the main text, may lightning strike the author's antenna! Oversimplification is our watchword.

Footnotes and appendices will have some additional technical detail for folks who are interested, but this is not intended as a treatise on wave theory. It will hit the minimums in the hopes that those will be most easily remembered and put into good, practical use by the reader.

Although many long-distance cruisers also carry and are licensed to use amateur radio (ham radio), there are many guides available for this more technical service. We'll defer to those guides and only touch on ham as it relates to marine frequency SSB operation, and in fact defer most discussion of SSB itself to a freely downloadable supplement so we're not cluttering up the place with complexity most readers will never need to understand.

CHAPTER ONE
The Radio System

Common Equipment, Uncommon Understanding

Most boats today come with a VHF radio, but most recreational boaters come into the community with little or no experience using one. Although radios are pervasive in modern daily living—everything from your cell phone to your car keys make use of RF (radio frequency) technology—most of those uses have been smoothed out and translated for an optimal consumer experience.

Not so with marine VHF! For reasons we will get into in a moment, it's a raw, unnatural experience for most boaters. If that includes you, it's understandable: your background isn't necessarily technical or nautical, and even if it was, you might be uncomfortable with public speaking... and there's nothing more public than blasting your voice out to the world with 25 watts behind it, reaching every vessel with a radio within 20 miles or so.

That may make you uncomfortable using what is one of the most powerful and versatile tools on your boat.

You likely picked up this book for any one of a number of reasons:

1. You feel nervous about broadcasting your voice to a large audience.
2. You don't have a strong command of the mechanics or processes of using radio equipment.
3. You don't know what to say or how to say it when hailing or receiving transmissions.

By helping you address point number 2, we think we can also help you with points number 1 and 3. If you learn the basic elements of how a VHF radio works (and how those elements affect the kinds of conversations and capabilities it supports), we think you'll be more comfortable using the technology. And by describing some of the customs and regulations that have grown up around radio use, and marine VHF radio use in particular, you can begin to wrap your head around both what you hear on your radio and how to take part in conversations while feeling like part of the larger community.

Guglielmo Marconi, the guy that made marine radio happen.

You have a fellow named Guglielmo Marconi to thank for all this. Around the turn of the century (no, not this one, the last one —1900ish), building on the work of a number of more theoretical scientists, Marconi transformed the maritime industry (and the world, really) by designing and building a network of shore and seagoing radio stations. For the first time, mariners could listen to one another brag about the size of the salmon they caught or rage at the inconsiderate wakes coming off passing vessels. But one or two good things came out of marine radio, too.

First and foremost, mariners in trouble suddenly gained the ability to call for assistance even when far from land or other vessels. It's well-known that a contributing factor in the *Titanic* disaster was the failure of the *Californian*, the closest vessel to the doomed liner on that fateful winter evening in 1912, to monitor her radio and respond to the distress calls; fewer people are aware that only a few years earlier, in 1909, upwards of 700 people were saved from the RMS *Republic* when that vessel summoned help after a collision off the Nantucket Shoals with her Marconi radio... the first time in history that a distress call from a vessel had ever been made.

Along the way, radio, and eventually today's mainstay of the in-shore commercial and recreational fleet, Very High Frequency (VHF) radio, has served the community in myriad ways.
- Prevented untold numbers of collisions and mishaps by allowing the easy communication of passing arrangements between vessels.
- Allowed up-to-date weather forecasts and warnings to be received.
- Kept boaters in touch with family and friends ashore or on other vessels.
- Expedited moorage arrangements and port operations.
- Smoothed out navigational matters such as transiting locks or passing through opening bridges.
- Kept folks apprised of where the fish are biting.

Although cell phones and satellite phones have become common, they still have not replaced VHF, and probably will not replace it anytime soon. The VHF system has a certain simplicity and ubiquity that makes it pretty hard to beat for safety and other short-range communications. With modern updates to that system, such as Digital Selective Calling, it even takes on some of the advantages of phones while retaining the versatility and universality that it already incorporates.

While the system has some limitations, the biggest one is simply that many people that have VHF radios don't really know how to use them. But we can change that! Keep reading.

Why VHF Is Hard

If you've ever wondered why talking on the radio seems so foreign, it pretty much comes down to just three things. The laws of the universe are conspiring against us here, so there's really no way around these limitations, but if you understand what they are, you will begin to see why radio hardware is put together as it is, and how many of the otherwise apparently ridiculous aspects of etiquette and protocol are designed to allow radio systems to function smoothly.

Transmission Range Is Limited

Although the limits are different between different frequency bands, all radio transmissions have limited range. Power falls off rapidly over distance, courtesy of the inverse square law.[1] The electromagnetic waves carrying your transmission thin out dramatically the further they travel. That means less signal is available to the receiver at greater ranges.

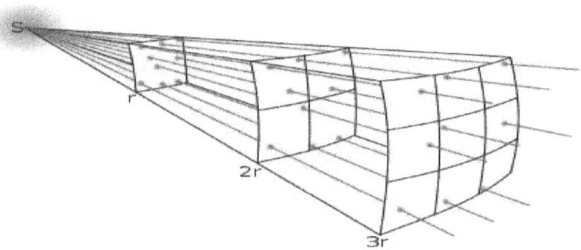

The Inverse Square Law in action... if the transmitter is at "S," you can see how the red signal dissipates at increasing distances.
Image by Borb, used under Creative Commons License [CC BY-SA 4.0 (https://creativecommons.org/licenses/by-sa/4.0)]

---

[1] The signal strength is inversely proportional to the square of the distance between the transmitter and the receiver, or $1 \propto 1/d^2$ for you mathematically minded folks. And yes, that's a mathematical equation, but it's not in the main text! :p

Because sound waves work basically the same way, you can think of transmitters as people standing around yelling at each other. The closer person will usually be the one you can hear unless the further one has a really loud voice. But as you can see from the diagram, the strength of the voice has to increase by quite a lot to overcome even relatively small increases in distance. Furthermore, in the case of VHF, the waves are basically restricted to traveling within the line of sight of the transmitter.

The upshot is that anyone close enough and loud enough is going to get through, while someone further away or quieter won't be heard.

Transmission Quality Is Poor

Even the best marine VHF transmission is never going to rival what you hear on your average FM car stereo every day. In part because of the ol' inverse square law up there, the strength of the signal just isn't going to be good enough most of the time to offer quality sound at the receiver. Although it's essentially the same type of transmission that you get from any big FM radio station, boats (and most shore stations) just don't have either the massive antenna setup or the kilowatts of power that those fixed-site transmitters leverage to pump out the signal.

Marine channel ranges are also more compressed than those for commercial FM stations, which means there is less bandwidth, and they carry a smaller frequency range.[2] In practice, that means the lower-pitch tones in your voice won't carry through, nor will subtleties of tone that you may commonly use to express yourself —basically, the channel can carry less information than what you are used to conveying in normal speech.

And as relatively weak electrical impulses flying through a capricious atmosphere and coursing down into an electromechanical environment that is practically designed to

---

[2] Frequency, in this sense, meaning the pitch of the tones in your voice, not the radio frequency itself.

create interference, those already inadequate signals are subject to static and interference. Pushing those sounds out through a cheap speaker that you'd be embarrassed to put in a Barbiemobile is a recipe for distortion and miscommunication.

Only One Person Can Talk At A Time

Marine VHF (and SSB, or Single Side-Band, which we'll also touch on lightly at times) are primarily simplex systems[3]. You don't care about the scientific origins of that term, but you do care about what it means: only one person can talk at a time!

You'll hear, as you are using the radio, moments where multiple transmitters try to talk at the same time, or "step on" each other. This is a fight about transmitting power and range. If you are not one of the stations involved, you can sometimes tell when this is happening—two people trying to have a conversation that neither of them can hear.

VHF has something called the capture effect, where the more powerful transmitter will tend to win out, and you won't hear the other at all. Often, however, the interference will garble what comes through.

If you are one of the transmitters that is interfering or being interfered with, you won't hear any of this competition. Your radio can only transmit, or only listen, not both simultaneously. As long as you are pushing the microphone button, you cannot receive.

This is a big part of the problem that people have conversing naturally on the radio, because it doesn't mimic any of our other normal conversations, either in person or by phone or computer. In fact, when most instruction booklets direct you to "speak

---

[3] As we'll discuss later, this is not universally true—in fact, both systems were originally designed for, and allocated, channels that work in *duplex* mode, which allows both parties to talk and listen simultaneously. For a variety of reasons, the duplex channels and capabilities have largely fallen out of use today (or, from the boater's point of view, operate identically to simplex systems). Also worth noting: some guides use simplex and duplex differently, with simplex referring to receive-only systems. We're following International Telecommunication Union (ITU) definitions in this text, as do most marine radio instruction guides.

normally" into the radio microphone, they're getting it absolutely wrong... normal just isn't allowed.

So these are the major limitations that govern your interactions on VHF radio. From them emerge the types of standards and practices that govern VHF usage. As we break it all down, though, you'll see a thread of logic and simplicity running through all of it, starting with the basic elements of your radio setup.

Making VHF Radio Understandable

Radio technology has been around for more than a hundred years now, but the same three basic bits that make up a radio are still the same:
- A radio
- An antenna
- Power

You're making a mistake if you think of your radio as just a chunk of plastic and metal with a flicker of electricity bringing it to life, though. No, a radio is just one piece of a much larger *system*—a collection of bunches of bits of plastic and metal charged up with electricity, yes, but also a set of standards of conduct and rules of use that govern how people use that equipment and interact.

> By far, the most complex part of the radio system is what happens over the air—the interaction between the users, both those actively engaged in conversation and the many inactive participants who are merely receiving.

You'll find that these interactions are guided by a combination of rules (some legal, some dictated by the laws of physics) and of common practices formed within the community. Both have developed around the limitations of radio technology.

Even an in-depth theoretical understanding of the physics and mechanics of radio transmission doesn't prepare you for participating in that system, so we're going to focus on the things that will: etiquette and protocol.

We're going to tackle this complexity in a 4-step process to help you break it down and understand it all:

1. **Building your radio listening skills** — Maybe seventy percent of the problem in using the radio comfortably for most people actually has little to do with talking; rather, they have trouble entering the conversation because they don't understand what they *hear* from other stations. We'll give you some exercises to train your ear and help you understand what you are hearing so you are more comfortable when replying to or initiating VHF conversations.
2. **Making sense of the overall radio system** — Part of understanding what you are hearing, as well as how to talk on the radio, is becoming comfortable with the conventions governing radio conversations. You'll learn both the formal and informal rules of VHF usage, and aspects of selecting channels, power levels, and other settings.
3. **Learning how to speak on the radio** — For all that most radio manuals exhort you to "speak normally" into the VHF microphone, the truth is that you need to pick up new habits and techniques to make yourself understood. Although these are far from natural, they can be learned, and we'll show you how to practice those skills.
4. **Picking up the tricks to sound like a pro** — Finally, once you get the basics down and begin to fully understand how radio conversations happen, you can start to adopt some more advanced techniques that will truly make you sound like a VHF pro.

Finally, we'll talk a little bit about radio technology... how things like the installation and configuration of your radio can affect your reception and transmissions. Although this isn't a technical manual, we'll get into some of the technical elements of troubleshooting when you run into problems that aren't just a case of nerves or misunderstandings.

Conventions

Although the book is primarily aimed at the vast majority of recreational users, who don't need and will never use the longer-range, and more complicated, SSB radio system, most of the basics of radio use apply equally to both systems, and we'll include some discussion of SSB (and its close cousin, ham radio) as a sort of gateway to that larger world of communication along the way. In general, this book (and a freely downloadable supplement specific to SSB and ham use) will simply use the term "radio" when talking about the common aspects of those systems and clarify differences by referring to them separately when necessary.

Similarly, there are many differences in design capability and regulatory aspects between installations transmitting from shore and vessels using the same spectrum. But there are few practical differences that recreational boaters would care about, so the book will use the generic term "station" to refer to both types of transmitters unless it becomes necessary to make a distinction.

As you go through the book, you'll find some text is formatted differently to emphasize or distinguish certain items of information.

> Callouts are just parts of the text that we want to draw attention to because they hold some particular importance or are worth extra emphasis.

```
Radio conversations will be shown in this
font and format.
```

We discuss phonetic spelling and the phonetic Latin alphabet in the Phonetics section, but we won't generally spell out the phonetic pronunciation of letters even when it is used in practice in the main text. For example, VHF channel 21A is pronounced "Two One Alpha." The exception will be in our example radio conversations, where the words will be spelled out as you would hear or say them on the radio.

Vessel names will be *italicized*.

And, after much angst and due debate and consideration, the abbreviation for microphone will be rendered as mike and not mic.[4]

---

[4] This more of a hot button debate than you might imagine, which is the only reason this sentence is even included. All parties agree that mike is the older and more traditional shortening of the word microphone, and is phonically compatible; the book's editor, however, and one of the early reviewers (a musician, and thus a member of the very group that likely corrupted this once right and honorable usage of the Queen's English) both informed me that mic was now the preferred form.

For a full philosophical and ecumenical cataloging of this larger dispute, you may visit the amusing and comprehensive web page devoted to the topic by Samuel Bayer here: https://sambayer.com/tirades/whymike.html

For the purposes of this book, mike wins because of what Sam says, and because I think mic looks funny anywhere but on a circuit diagram.

CHAPTER TWO
Listening

Developing Listening Skills

To borrow and bastardize a famous Yogi Berra quote, you can hear a lot just by listening.

For new or casual radio users, just understanding the noises coming out of the box can be a significant challenge. Shot-through with static, distorted by limited vocal frequency range, characterized by clipped language and jargon, tuning into marine radio channel for the first time is like accidentally hitting scan on your car radio and ending up on the local Spanish-language station. ¡Viva!

There are two reasons that you need to tackle this problem before you can become a proficient radio user:

1. First, you have to be able to hear and understand transmissions that are coming across in order to have a conversation. Otherwise, you're like the deaf guy at the party: answering questions that weren't asked and asking questions that have already been answered.[5]
2. Second, the best way to learn common use is just by paying attention to how other people are talking. It's like picking up any language—your brain will hear it and start to make sense of the patterns the longer you listen.

Listening skills are critical to radio use.

Just getting started with listening in can be a problem for several different reasons, though:

- The speakers in radios are famously bad; tiny, underpowered, and inconveniently located, most stock speakers don't deliver clear sound reproduction.
- Interference is common.

---

[5] Considering the demographics of American boaters, you probably *are* that deaf guy at the party.

- Radios are often poorly located. Sailboaters, for example, have a terrible reputation for monitoring their radios when underway. This is usually because the sailor is, appropriately, up in the cockpit, while the radio is, traditionally, located below at the nav station.[6]

Like any other skill, listening takes practice. Of course, you should have your radio on and pay attention any time you are underway, but there are often many opportunities to listen in even if you aren't going anywhere. Working on the engine at the marina some afternoon? Flip on the VHF and listen to the traffic. Anchored out with nothing else going on some lazy summer evening? Turn on the radio for free entertainment.

> Gradually, through listening, your ear will tune itself to understand radio transmissions.

These occasions are also your chance to play around a little and check in on some channels you might not otherwise monitor. In areas where mandatory Vessel Traffic Service (VTS) schemes are in use, it's a good idea to monitor them when underway... but if you don't have multiple radios or a radio that supports scanning, that's not always possible. But sitting at the dock, you can listen in to commercial traffic and learn how the big boys do it.

Listening Without a Radio

Nor are you restricted to listening when you are on board. If you have, or are willing to pick up, a simple radio scanner, you can monitor the air from just about anywhere. Of course, if you don't live near the water, you won't pick up marine VHF.

---

[6] More on this common deficiency and how to address it can be found in the Radio Installation section toward the end of the book.

Online Marine Radio Traffic

But the miracle of the modern Internet can fix that—sites such as Broadcastify stream audio from other people with scanners all over the country, focused on every imaginable band, including marine traffic.

Even the busiest marine radio frequencies are relatively sedate, however. You can find examples that other folks have already picked out and recorded and uploaded on YouTube (usually distress calls), and Broadcastify archives streams for a certain amount of time, so you can go back and listen to certain stations during a period you think likely to be interesting.

Public Safety Nets

For other examples of good radio practice and procedure, you can expand your horizons. Police and fire bands are used routinely and heavily, and both dispatchers and officers quickly become proficient in radio use. When it's a matter of life and death, people tend to rapidly pick up the tricks necessary to get their messages across clearly and quickly.

Of course, police and fire use has a different pattern and feel to it from marine traffic, but spotting the differences and thinking about them is equally informative. On the other hand, the users often share a military background with the Coast Guard and commercial vessel crews you will hear on marine frequencies, so there will be some overlap in pro words and other practices.

Air Traffic Control

If you want a graduate-level course in radio use that is almost entirely unlike marine traffic, tune into the airline bands. The patter between professional pilots and air traffic controllers is honed through hundreds of interactions per day, on busy channels, with breathtaking consequences for misunderstandings. You will not find faster or more compressed conversations. At first, you won't even be able to understand them. But they are perfectly comprehensible, even routine, to the people making them.

If you think marine radio is difficult, try hanging with these guys for a while!
Via the Asian Military Review

Making Sense of Patterns

If you choose to listen to police, fire, or other regular radio traffic, you will start to notice how they shorten their broadcasts by liberal uses of code, slang, and shorthand. There has been a trend in recent years to move away from obscure codes like the old APCO[7] 10 codes toward more natural language—it's both easier to understand without intensive training and easier to recall in stressful situations. But despite that, you'll still notice that dispatchers and officers liberally sprinkle their transmissions with terms like "Code 4" for "everything is okay" or "I'm going on a seven" for "I'm going to be taking a break and will be

---

[7] The Association of Public-Safety Communications Officials, the folks who brought you "10-4, good buddy." Ten codes were designed to abbreviate transmissions in an era when police might have only a single channel to cover an entire city. Interestingly, the "10" part is meaningless, designed to insert a dead syllable at the front of a transmission, which is otherwise likely to be cut off or garbled. You'll note elsewhere in the book we suggest you train yourself to key your microphone a half-second before speaking, for the same reason.

unavailable." Street names are chopped up—"3 and Vine" instead of "Third and Vine." Instead of completing a query in certain situations, like "Medic 10, are you ready to copy patient information?" a dispatcher might just say "Medic 10." And because of the context, the medic unit will acknowledge and be ready to take down the data.

All of this is possible because of a shared protocol. By understanding when certain phrases are expected and the context of the conversation, the users are able to dramatically shorten it.

This level of shared understanding is not possible in the marine environment, but the protocol that governs radio use on the water nonetheless has many of the same characteristics.

Radio protocol provides a shared context for making assumptions about what will be in a transmission, which assists in understanding that transmission even when some of the elements are removed by static or interference.

Using Your New Listening Skills

Honing your listening skills will serve you in two ways:
- You'll tune your ear to better understand the sometimes garbled and faint radio calls coming in from other stations.
- Your brain will start to pick up the patterns and protocols that are inherent in those conversations and begin to internalize them.

The human brain is actually really good at mimicry—it's how you learned to speak in the first place. So simply exposing it to radio traffic will help it start to mimic the patterns that will make you sound like a natural when you make calls yourself.

You can take this a step further by actually repeating what you hear to yourself right after you have heard it. Just mumble the lines under your breath, just as you heard them. Although it sounds a little silly, you're actually training yourself to talk that way—your brain is adapting itself by practicing the lines.

Making Sense of Radio Language

Once you've started listening more regularly, you should eventually begin to distinguish words and sentences coming out of the squawk box. But almost immediately you'll run into another problem: although you will recognize them as good, respectable English words, the way they are put together won't make any sense!

That's because you aren't yet familiar with the rules and rituals with which those transmissions are put together. Although it may sound like mere chaos at the moment, there are some solid, sensible rules that you can learn to help it all snap into place.

Protocol: Not Just A Pointless Set Of Rules

If you're like most people, you probably think of radio protocols as being some sort of archaic military convention or a pastime for pedantic nerds. But there is a point to all the "Roger, 10-4, over and out,"[8] stuff that goes beyond military machismo and has a real and vital purpose for radio communications, even in civilian use.

These protocols all make sense if you keep a few of the realities of radio conversations in mind:
- There are a limited number of channels
- The channels are susceptible to interference
- Usually, only one party can talk on one channel at a time (simplex)
- Everyone on a channel can hear everyone else talking within range (party line)

Viewed from that perspective, you can see that most radio procedures are therefore designed to:
- Limit the amount of air time required to communicate

---

[8] Please don't ever actually say this on the radio. Or anywhere. And if you do, please don't tell anyone you own this book.

- Increase the clarity of those communications

It is true, however, that much of modern radio protocol has largely been created by and shaped on military radio nets. Each branch, and even various elements within those branches, has its own radio culture of a sort, with slightly different habits and connotations.

U.S. Marine Corps photo by Angel Serna/Released

These, in turn, leak out into law enforcement and civilian radio nets as former military operators return to civilian life and bring their habits with them.

By far, the biggest influence on the culture of marine radio is the active-duty Coast Guard. Much of the traffic you hear on a VHF radio on an average day on the water near any busy recreational port will be from Coast Guard watchstanders and craft. And this, in turn, shapes how civilian marine radio operators converse over the air.

You can trace some of this influence through various tics that don't have any apparent place in civilian conversation, such as the habit of using "say again…" instead of "repeat."

There's no particular reason to reject the use of the word "repeat" in civilian life—it's not easily confused with any similar word and it's certainly more concise.

But in military use, "repeat" has a very specific meaning, an important one having to do with coordinating artillery fire. That's not the sort of thing you want to mess up with live ammunition, so military radio operators have it drummed into them to use "say again" instead.

And that's what you'll hear on the water, even though artillery fire does not feature prominently in the average recreational boating trip.

"Repeat" is one example of what is called a pro word, or procedure word.[9]

> Pro words are words that are restricted for use on the radio in only a single context, to eliminate the possibility of being misunderstood.

You can find a list of these words in the Pro Words section.

Pro words are just one aspect of the radio system that can make it difficult and intimidating to pick up. But there is a point to them—they contain mutually agreed-upon meanings that are useful and unique, and they have been chosen for phonemes that are easy to recognize even in a low-quality or broken transmission.

Learning those words and understanding the protected uses will help you understand the conversations you hear and help keep you from making mistakes when you start chatting on the

---

[9] "Repeat" and "Say Again" are also great examples of pro words being less-than-universal; in commercial marine use, as recommended by the IMO's Standard Marine Communication Phrases, "repeat" is the preferred nomenclature for indicating that you will be, well, repeating a segment of your transmission. "Say Again" is used only as a request for another station to re-transmit information.

radio yourself.

Radio Use Is Shaped By Custom and Regulation

A bit like driving, radio use is shaped by both customs *and* regulations. Some acts are proscribed; others are just habits that are broadly understood and expected by the community of users.

On the regulation side, every country is entitled to manage its own radio spectrum, so if you head off into exotic foreign waters (say, Canada), you may find different rules. For instance, you'll find that channel use and frequencies are allocated differently. This is reflected in the fact that marine VHF radios usually come out of the box with three different channel plan settings:

- U.S.
- Canadian
- International

You may encounter other regulatory differences between countries, including:

- How stations are required to identify themselves
- What channels may be used for what purposes
- Whether or not a license is required

It's not as chaotic as it sounds. International treaties (such as Chapter 4 of the 1974 SOLAS treaty)[10] govern some radio practices (such as the restriction of channel 16 or 2182 kHz for hailing or distress purposes), and the International Maritime Organization (IMO) and International Telecommunications Union (ITU) publish and maintain standards such as the International Radio Regulations[11] and Standard Marine Communications

---

[10] IMO. "International convention for the safety of life at sea (SOLAS)." London 1 November 1974. UN Treaty Series vol. 1184 p. 278 (1974).

[11] "Radio Regulations." International Telecommunications Union, 2016.

Phrases[12] to offer guidance to national agencies and international shipping. You'll find that common custom ensures that many others line up more or less like you're used to. After all, radio is about communication, and you can't communicate if you're not on the same wavelength.[13]

Beyond the regulations, there are also varying customs in different regions or countries. The degree of formality in protocol, the amount of time that people allow others when they are hailing, even the sorts of subjects that may or may not be considered proper to conduct over the air can all change from community to community. You'll even find that the use and meaning of some pro words can vary in different regions.

Because of that, and because they are rarely written out or articulated, these aspects of protocol can be the hardest to pick up and the most likely to make you uncomfortable using the radio.

So we're going to break down the most basic elements of a radio conversation for you and explain not only how it is supposed to work, but why.

---

[12] IMO Sub-Committee on Safety of Navigation, and Rijeka College of Maritime Studies. "IMO Standard Marine Communication Phrases." International Maritime Organization. April 4, 2000, NAV46/INF.4 edition, sec. Agenda Item 9.

[13] That's a little radio-related humor for you there. Get it?

PROWORDS

These lists of procedure words aren't comprehensive, but they are the ones you will most commonly hear in the marine environment. You might note others that are common in your region

Distress Pro words

Mayday	Indicates the broadcast is an emergency; reserves the air
Mayday Relay	Used to pass along an emergency broadcast
Pan Pan	Indicates the broadcast is regarding an urgent message
Received Mayday	Acknowledges that a Mayday message has been received
Seelonce Mayday	Restricts channel to emergency traffic only
Seelonce Feenee	Ends the emergency restriction on the channel
Prudonce	Indicates that the channel can be used prudently for non-emergency traffic

Other Pro words

Acknowledge	Instructs the recipient of the message to positively respond they have received it
Affirmative	A positive confirmation; "yes"
Break	Indicates additional transmission from the same station will immediately follow, separate from the current transmission
Copy	Indicates the previous transmission has been received and understood
Correction	Indicates an error was made in the transmission and will continue with the correct information instead
Disregard	Cancels the information included in the current transmission
Negative	A negative confirmation; "no"
Read Back	Requests that the recipient read back, word for word, the transmission they have just received
Over	Indicates the current transmission is over and the other station in the conversation can now broadcast; a response is expected
Out	Used to close out the conversation and open the air up to other traffic
Securité	Indicates that the transmission includes safety and information content
This Is	Identifies the station calling
Roger/Received	Acknowledges receipt of the last transmission

Elements of a Radio Conversation

Every marine radio conversation that you hear (and, later, participate in) should follow the same basic pattern:

A radio user takes temporary control of the channel to make a call to another user or an announcement by:
- Pushing down the microphone button
- Starting the conversation with the name of the station they are calling or using a procedure word for an announcement
- Identifying themselves by stating their own boat or station name
- Saying "over" and releasing the microphone button

The "over" pro word announces that the air is temporarily turned over to someone else — the station being called. If they reply, then:
- They will identify themselves, say "over" when they are finished speaking, and release the microphone button
- The conversation will continue with exchanges following that same pattern until it's finished.
- Each party will say "out" instead of over on their last line

This pattern exists for a reason. The reality of a shared, one-way-only medium dictates that users of a channel signal their intentions to one another. Just keying the mike and starting to talk is one signal; obviously, you're grabbing the channel and trying to communicate with someone. You've taken control of the air, and until you relinquish it with the proper pro words, no one should interrupt.

But what next? How do other users know who you want to

talk to and when it's okay to talk themselves?
Protocol is designed to clear this up for everyone involved.

Who's In The Conversation?

Unless you are making a general call (such as a Mayday or Securité), the first word out of your mouth should be the name of the station that you are calling. Placing this first saves everyone time—every station *not* with that name can stop listening at that point.[14]

The next phrase should be your own vessel's name; that tells everyone who is making the call.

No one else is invited to the conversation—by putting those two names out there and initiating the conversation, you have claimed the channel temporarily for yourselves (unless you later call a third party into the conversation, which is perfectly acceptable).

The last word before you let the mike key go should be "over." This tells the other party that you are turning their channel "over" to them so they can reply. The two of you will volley control of the air back and forth through the entire conversation.

Eventually, that conversation is going to be finished. When you do not plan to transmit again, you will say "out" at the end of the sentence *instead* of "over."[15]

---

[14] Although you might need to do this under certain conditions or circumstances (say, when a multiparty conversation is going on), it's not necessary to identify the stations each time you transmit during a conversation, even if you switch channels.

[15] The film standard "over and out" is redundant; once you are "out" it is obvious that the air is turned "over" to anyone else who wants to use it.

A Typical Conversation

We'll be using a similar format to show examples of radio conversations throughout the remainder of the book, each illustrating a different kind of goal or situation you might have to handle. But just to cleanse the palate, so to speak, we'll start you off with a fairly typical and easily understood conversation that you might overhear or engage in by VHF sometime.

As with the remainder of our examples, for recreational boats we're going to pretend that your vessel name is *Serenity* and that the other boat in the conversation is named *Velcro*.

Setting the Scene

Radio conversations don't just happen randomly. You, or the party hailing you, will have a goal, and that will dictate many of the conventions and settings behind the transmission. We'll talk about those considerations in a later section, Speaking, in considerable detail. For now, you can assume that this conversation comes up as your boat, *Serenity*, is coming up astern of a slower vessel, *Velcro*, which is currently proceeding near the center of a narrow channel with branches on both sides. You aren't sure of *Velcro's* intentions but would like to pass her and be on your way.

Sounds like it's time for a quick radio conversation.

(On channel 16)
`Velcro, Velcro, Velcro, this is Serenity, Serenity, Serenity, over.`

(After about 20 seconds—maybe *Velcro's* skipper didn't get his coffee this morning)
`Ah... vessel calling Velcro, this is Velcro, go ahead.`

(Obviously he didn't catch your boat's name, either; you'd better make sure to repeat it for him)

Hello *Velcro*, this is *Serenity*, the 40-foot Bayliner just astern of you. I'd like to get around you here, passing on your port side, if that's alright, skipper.

Ahhh... *Serenity*, let's go up to 68, over.

Roger, 68.

(You switch your radio over to channel 68 and hail Velcro again)

Velcro, Serenity.

Serenity, roger... I'm planning to enter the channel off to port coming up here in about 200 yards, so I'd prefer you pass me on my starboard side. I'll shift my course to port for you, but there's a large tug coming up on my port bow here, so it will be a couple of minutes before I can do that, over.

(Well, these things can't be helped; you don't mind waiting as long as no one gets turned into bug-splatter on the bow of a tug.)

Velcro, I copy that, and that's no problem... I'll wait for you to shift your course to port and then pass on your starboard side. Much appreciated. *Serenity* back to 16.

Roger that, *Velcro* out.

Now, this conversation has been artificially adjusted to be more complex than it would probably be in real life; a channel change wouldn't typically happen unless both of you are uncommonly courteous and other traffic was happening on 16. *Velcro* might just slow down and hug the starboard side of the lane and let you take your chances head-on with the tug. And you could simply use sound signals to accomplish essentially the same task.

But it's also less complex than it might be, as well. You might not get hold of *Velcro* on your first try; he might be hard to hear; the arrangements might fall apart if the oncoming tug does something unexpected. So this is a reasonable, middle-of-the-road example of a radio conversation you might have or hear in any well-trafficked waterway in North America on a weekend afternoon. You'll note that it both follows and breaks the protocol we've described in places… keep reading to find out why!

Following the Rules

Everything you have heard on the radio has involved some combination of customs and regulations. It's not worth breaking down the distinction in most cases since the point is clear: cooperation and clarity in communication to make the best use of a shared, limited resource (bandwidth).

But there are other aspects of radio use that are primarily regulatory that must be followed when you are using a marine radio:

- No foul language
- Identify yourself
- Conversations must involve operational matters, even on working channels
- Without a special station license, you may not use a marine radio on land (a handheld VHF, for example)

Breakin' The Law

You don't have to listen long to find out that many of these regulations are frequently broken. And with some of them, there is a lot of gray area involved... what exactly is an "operational matter," for example? Coordinating a passing maneuver obviously qualifies; how about sharing tips about a hot fishing spot? No one will call you to account for that. But if you are hogging channel 68 talking about your favorite episode of "Vikings," you are probably breaking the law... and certainly being rude.

Fake distress calls might top the list of no-nos, for obvious reasons. Disturbingly, they also seem to be one of the most common violations.

There are also technical violations to consider. Exceeding authorized transmitting power or using a false Maritime Mobile Service Identity (MMSI) number[16] are also illegal and subject to

---

[16] For more about MMSI numbers, see the Appendix: Decoding MMSI Numbers and the Digital Selective Calling sections of the book.

the same punishments as willful misuse.

Penalties

A fake distress call is serious business, and the penalties are severe:
- Up to six years in prison
- A $250,000 criminal fine
- Additional fines up to $5,000 per hour for rescue-related expenses

Apart from distress hoaxes, prosecutions for rules violations are unusual. The FCC can cite or warn you, however, resulting in fines or the loss of radio privileges, or even jail time:
- Up to $16,000 in fines on the first offense
- Up to one year in prison

Whether they can find you to issue the citation is another question! In cases of persistent abuse, radio-direction finding apparatuses have been used to track down violators. It's also possible, or maybe even likely, that other irritated users nearby will find a way to identify you and turn you in.

Licensing

Do you need a license to use marine radio? If you've researched your responsibilities online regarding marine radio use, you probably ran across a lot of conflicting information about whether or not you need a license to use a VHF or SSB.

Much of this confusion is due to context,[17] but the Coast Guard website clears it up nicely:

> An FCC ship station radio license is no longer required for any vessel traveling in U.S. waters which uses a VHF marine radio, radar or EPIRB, and which is not required to carry radio equipment. A license is necessary however for any vessel required to carry a marine radio, on an international voyage, or carrying an HF single sideband radiotelephone or marine satellite terminal.

There are two different licenses you may have to obtain:

Ship Station License

Since recreational craft are not required to carry radio equipment (they are "voluntary ships" in the FCC vernacular) unless they are power-driven vessels exceeding 20 meters in length on navigable waterways or certificated, that pretty much leaves licensing to:

---

[17] As implied by the Coast Guard quote, you USED TO have to have a ship station license for any radio installation, but that rule was changed in 1996. If you are looking at older resources they may not reflect the current regime. Also, the Coast Guard and the FCC define "passenger-carrying vessels" slightly differently, which has created some confusion in the past.

- Whether you plan to travel internationally[18]
- Whether or not you install an SSB

If you do need a ship station license, you can apply online or using paper forms available on the FCC's website.

As implied by the name, the license is to the ship. If you buy another vessel, you will have to reapply for a new license for that boat.

Restricted Radiotelephone Operator's Permit

This is an individual, lifetime license that allows you to operate VHF internationally or marine SSB on a properly licensed ship's station. Like the ship station license, there is no test—you only have to apply and pay the fee. And like the ship station license, it's only required if you are using an SSB or traveling internationally.

- Forms 159 and 605 are required for both types of licenses and can be filed electronically or the old-fashioned way. Both forms are available on the FCC website. Or, you can apply online at http://wireless.fcc.gov.
- You will also have to file Form 605 if you sell your vessel to cancel the ship station license—it does not go to the new owner.
- Renewals are due every 10 years for ship station licenses. The FCC is supposed to send you a reminder 120 days before the renewal is due, but there is no grace period—if you miss the renewal date for any reason, you will have to reapply.

Amateur Radio Licensing

Amateur radio, or ham, which partly overlaps coverage of MF/HF marine bands, has a separate licensing scheme. There are several considerations involved with choosing between the two,

---

[18] Actually, technically, whether or not you plan to ever contact a foreign station, even from U.S. waters... transmitting to a vessel in Mexican waters requires that you have a ship station license.

however:
- Amateur licenses (and radios) offer access to more bands, which increases the chances of getting a good signal out in marginal conditions.
- Amateur licensing requires that you pass tests.
- Even with an amateur license, you do not have access to all marine bands.
- Your amateur license will not cover marine VHF operation internationally.

More information about ham licenses is available in the freely downloadable SSB supplement to this book, available at http://marineradio.forlubbers.com/.

CHAPTER THREE
Speaking

Fitting the Format to Your Need

Before you can learn how to talk on the radio, you need to know what it is that you are going to talk *about*.

There are different protocols, channels, and procedures to follow for different types of conversations. Finding the right format to fit your needs is going to be the first step in making yourself more comfortable with speaking on the radio because you will understand what the expectations are for other listeners, as well as where to find them.

In this chapter, we'll lay out the major protocols that you will use to make contact and conduct a conversation over your VHF, but first, we're going to lay out what the choices are, how to set up your radio for those conversations, and offer some examples of situations in which a particular protocol might apply.

Hailing Another Vessel/Shore Station
- **Some Examples:**
    - You want to ask about weather or water conditions in a nearby area
    - You are trying to find a friend on their boat nearby
    - You need to arrange to stay at a marina for the night
- **Channel:** Usually 16, 9, or 13, but others are possible.
- **Power:** Depends
- **Protocol:** Hailing and Answering

This is the bread and butter stuff of every day VHF use... getting ahold of another station, either afloat or ashore, for any sort of non-emergency communications.

Safety Broadcasts
- **Some Examples:**
    - You are about to enter a narrow channel and want to ask that other vessels avoid you during your transit
    - You are having steering or engine problems and can't control your boat as normal

- You are operating in heavy fog and believe other boats may be nearby
- **Channel:** Channels 16 or 13
- **Power:** Depends
- **Protocol:** Securité

Safety broadcasts involve essential communications to coordinate between vessels operating in the same area that may not be clear under the conventional rules-of-the-road... basically any time you need a little extra elbow room and want to ask vessels around you to watch out with more care than usual.

Distress and Assistance Requests
- **Some Examples:**
    - Your engine has gone out, and you are unable to make port
    - Someone on your boat has been injured
    - You have a fire on board
    - Weather conditions have suddenly turned extreme, and you believe you may not be safe on your boat
- **Channel:** 16
- **Power:** High
- **Protocol:** Assistance/Urgency/Distress

Although these are the least common types of radio communication, they are the most important—how you get help and assistance when you need it.

The next section will go into a little more detail about channels, their uses, and the power level and other settings you will want to check before you have a radio conversation.

Choosing What Type of Call To Make When You Need Help

As we'll discuss later, you have a lot of options for getting help with your radio. To the uninitiated, a Mayday is basically the only option, because it's the only one they know exists.

But that's often like booking yourself in for a quadruple bypass when experiencing a little bit of heartburn. Not knowing your radio options can either cause you to overreact when you need help, or to avoid asking for it entirely, possibly leading to a much worse situation.

You can think of these options as running along a continuum, from the easiest and least intensive all the way up to full-blown, helicopter-flying, siren-blaring emergencies. You're still responsible for figuring out the right call to make, but just knowing the menu can help.

Channels and Setup

Everything you hear when you turn on the radio is just the tip of the iceberg. There is a chain of decisions being made before you even press the transmit button, and you need to understand what those factors are before starting up a radio conversation.

The mechanics of doing this will vary from radio to radio, and we'll talk more about those details in later chapters. For now, if you come across a setting you don't recognize or understand, you can fast-forward to the Operations and Troubleshooting section for more information.

Picking the Channel For VHF Calls

One big decision that has to be made before making a transmission is deciding what channel to make it on. For obvious reasons, only people on that channel will hear the traffic, irrespective of range, power, and other factors.

Fortunately, there is a logical hierarchy and plan for channel use in most areas.

We'll go into more detail about VHF channels and frequencies later on, but the truth is that most recreational boaters only use, or need to think about, a handful of channels.

Some of these are called hailing channels, and that's their primary purpose—for vessels to connect with each other. Because many radios only listen in on a single channel at a time, for anyone to get in touch with anyone else, there needs to be prior agreement about what channel that will be.[19]

The default hailing channel for VHF is usually Channel 16. Most recreational and commercial vessels monitor this frequency by law, so it's usually the best place to start.

But that's not always true. In some situations, the station you

---

[19] This is becoming less and less true as more radios are built with scanning functions (discussed later in the text) and since a technology called DSC is obviating the need for traditional hailing channels entirely, but, legally and practically, this is still how it is handled for the most part.

are looking for will be on a different channel.
- **Channel 13** — This is the designated ITU (International Telecommunication Union) bridge-to-bridge[20] working channel for internship safety. All vessels over 20 meters are required to maintain a listening watch while underway. Also, actual bridges, the kind that carry roads and rails over channels and rivers, usually monitor Channel 13, as do most locks. Your Local Notice to Mariners (we'll tell you more about this later) or signs posted on shore or the bridges themselves will usually list other channels if this standard is not used.
- **Channel 9** — On the East Coast, Channel 9 is encouraged as a hailing channel in place of Channel 16 for recreational craft.
- **VTS Channels** — Mandatory Vessel Traffic Service[21] is in place in the waters approaching certain busy U.S. and Canadian ports. As a matter of course, vessels participating in those schemes are not required to monitor Channel 16 as long as they are available on the designated VTS channel.
- **Custom local channels** — Some regions adopt their own channels as a de facto community line. Channel 6, for example, on the West Coast of Vancouver Island, is the channel that most local vessels and resorts monitor. And marinas throughout B.C. have agreed to listen on Channel 66, to keep the evening conversations about moorage from cluttering up Channel 16. You can find similar regional norms anywhere in the world.

---

[20] That's bridge as in "The captain's on the bridge" and not bridge as in "The car is on the bridge."

[21] Maintained by their respective Coast Guards or cooperatively with local agencies, you can find links to North American VTS schemes and their respective radio channel and monitoring regulations here: https://www.navcen.uscg.gov/?pageName=vtsMain

Selecting a Working Channel

Because an extended discussion on most designated hailing channels would tie them up and prevent others from using them, you also need to plan on a channel to move the conversation to if you are successful in raising your target. These are called working channels, and several are set aside for different purposes.[22] You can find a complete list in the Appendix: VHF Frequency Plans. In the United States and Canada, recreational vessel-to-vessel working channels are:

- 68
- 69
- 71
- 72
- 78A

Note that some regions may offer up additional channels; 79 and 80 are available on the Great Lakes, for instance. Check the channel plan in the appendix for specifics for your area.

There are also working channels for other purposes that you might use for traffic that is not recreational in nature. For instance, the U.S. and Canadian Coast Guards each have preferred working channels set aside for conversations they are involved in. Various VTS schemes also maintain working channels for vessels they are handling. In those cases, you'll be told what that channel is if it's necessary to shift from the hailing frequency.

Set Your Power

As we'll discuss further in VHF Operation, you'll find that radios come with variable power settings. The amount of power behind your transmission will affect how far away it will be heard. If you know your intended target is nearby—or even if you just suspect they might be—the responsible thing to do is to set

---

[22] While some channels are explicitly designated as hailing channels, the lines are more blurry with others; VTS channels are typically used for both purposes, as is bridge-to-bridge (Channel 13). Because they are dual-use, you'll want to consider keeping even working conversations brief and to the point.

your power to low mode (1 watt). This will ensure that your conversation doesn't create more of a footprint than it needs to, and keeps the air free for other users.

If you don't reach your target on the first try, then by all means up the power on subsequent attempts—it could be you're not getting them because you're not getting through.

Note that on some channels, you may be restricted by both law and your radio settings to low power mode. Radios generally respect these restrictions in the hardware these days—if you're not allowed to transmit on high power, it won't let you.

Set Your Squelch

You should also consider checking your squelch setting before you start chatting. Squelch will be discussed in more detail later, but it's basically a sensitivity setting that determines at what level your radio will activate the speaker. Set too low, any random bit of static that hits the antenna will come blaring out at you; too high, and you won't even hear someone sitting right next to you at the dock transmitting.

One of the fastest ways to find a working squelch setting is to pick a channel with a continuous broadcast—a weather station works just fine—that is coming in at an acceptable level of clarity. That is to say, it's not so far away that you hear it with a lot of drop-outs or distortions.

Turn your squelch all the way off (you will hear static even on an inactive channel at this setting) then tune to the broadcasting channel. You should hear it coming in normally. Slowly turn up the squelch setting to the point where the transmission starts dropping out... then nudge it just back to where everything is clear again.

If you're trying to reach a station that is far away or might otherwise have a weak signal, then you should select for more sensitivity. If you can find a broadcast station that is similarly weak, you can use it as your control level. Or just use the strong signal, but drop the squelch level further than it needs to be from that level. You'll get more transient static and broken transmissions, but on the plus side, you'll be able to hear responses from stations that are further away that would otherwise be lost.

Hailing and Answering

There are at least two sides to every radio conversation: the caller and the responder. You need to be prepared to take on either role.

Making a Radio Call

There is a specific format to making a call, or hailing, another station. The first step is: **Listen!**

You don't want to intrude on another conversation. Hailing channels are not supposed to be used for long conversations, but there is a chance that the Coast Guard is busy talking to someone or that someone else is in the middle of their own hailing call. After you tune your channel, listen in for 15-20 seconds and make sure no one else is in the middle of a conversation.

In a perfect world, you will also check your working channel before making the call to ensure someone else isn't already holding a long conversation over there. But this is not always possible, or sometimes you simply get pre-empted when someone else gets there in the middle of the process (we'll talk about what to do in those cases below.)

If everything appears clear, then make your own call.

The essence of every transmission can be wrapped up in the following four steps. Well, three, if you're one of those people who remembers to breathe on their own normally.

- **Think about what you need to communicate** — What essential information needs to go across in this particular transmission.
- **Rehearse it in your head** — Think for a moment about the

exact words you are going to use. Say it to yourself once or twice; not enough to get worked up, but enough to be sure that what you are going to say matches what you need to communicate. We'll talk about this more in just a minute!
- **Take a deep breath** — You don't want to run out of air mid-sentence. A lot of people forget to breathe!
- **Key the mike and hold** - Press the microphone button and hold it down for a half-second to a second before you begin speaking; otherwise, you may cut off the first word you say.

And don't forget to let up on the mike button when you're done!

Each of those four elements is important **every time you transmit.** Whether you are replying to someone else or starting the conversation, every time you key the mike, run through those same four steps. It doesn't matter if you have to pause for second first—it's worth it! In time, you'll do all four automatically and without thinking about it. For now, you might post them next to the radio so you don't forget.

The format for the initial call is ironclad: always put the name of the vessel you are calling FIRST, and identify your own vessel SECOND.

Velcro, Velcro, Velcro, this is *Serenity, Serenity, Serenity,* over.

Then—and this is sometimes a challenge—you wait. Not everyone is sitting on top of their radio all the time. It can take a while to get an answer. Be patient. It's going to seem like water torture, but you should give it at least a minute before trying again. Think about it: what are the odds that someone who wasn't listening five seconds ago is suddenly paying attention now? If they were in the head or hauling in a fish, it's gonna take them a minute. Incessant repetition on your part in no way speeds that process—you're just wasting airwaves.

If you repeat the call three times—at the appropriate interval!—with no answer, it's time to give up for a while. But you don't just go silent... when you started the process of making your call, you were taking control of that channel! Other responsible users, listening in before proceeding with their own traffic, have been holding off and waiting for the vessel you are calling to answer.

To open the air back up to those other users, you finish off the process by saying:

This is *Serenity*, no response heard, out.

This both clears the air for other users, and if for some reason your target heard you and replied, but you didn't receive them, it lets them know that you couldn't hear them. Hopefully, you bought them a copy of this book, and they can start the troubleshooting process to figure out why!

Calling a Target Without a Name
All radio calls, with the exception of a Mayday call, must be directed at someone.

Sometimes it happens that you want to have a chat with a vessel that you don't know the name of. Maybe there is a tug overtaking you, and you can't make out the name on the bow. Or you see a nearby cruiser out fishing from their tender, and you want to know if anything is biting. Or maybe it's a general call for assistance, or a query about conditions in a particular area—you don't care who answers.

In those cases, you can try them by using a combination of location and description. The location can also be a combination of absolute and relative... in other words, related to your own vessel and to some fixed geographic point:

Tug with the red funnel overtaking a

white 46-foot Bayliner off West Point, this is *Serenity*, *Serenity*, over.

Or just geographic, if the description is distinctive enough:

White dinghy with a blue stripe fishing on the west side of Mitlenatch Island, this is *Serenity*, *Serenity*, *Serenity*, over.

Or:

Any vessel in Seaforth Channel, this is *Serenity*, *Serenity*, looking for a fog report, over.

And if you are far from other references, an approximate position will often work:

Tanker in position 48 degrees, 15.2 minutes West, 126 degrees 1 minute North, this is the *Serenity*, 46-foot Bayliner 4 miles north of you, over.

Usually, a combination of specific description and location, combined with signal strength—a loud and clear voice indicates someone nearby—will get their attention.

On the other hand, don't be *too* generic. Hailing "Sailboat at the entrance to Fisherman's Bay" on a busy weekend afternoon in the San Juan Islands is basically a waste of time and airwaves. Find something descriptive enough to let your target know exactly who they are, or don't bother with the call.

For general calls, you can simply address them to "All

stations."

> Securité, Securité, Securité. All stations, all stations, all stations, this is *Serenity, Serenity, Serenity. Serenity* is a 46-foot Bayliner about to enter Dodd Narrows heading northbound. Any concerned or opposing traffic, please contact *Serenity* on 16, out.

Or if you're looking for someone in a certain area:

> Any station in the vicinity of Mitlenatch Island, this is *Serenity* calling, over.

DSC Calling

If you are using a radio equipped with Digital Selective Calling, the process is much simpler... assuming your target also has DSC, and you know their MMSI number.

If those things are all true and you know what that number is, all you have to do is punch it into your radio control panel, along with a choice of working channel. The system will ring the radio on the other end, and put both of you on the same channel to begin talking when they answer. It's just like making a phone call.[23]

Channel Considerations

For the most part, all of the above formats make no mention of the channel you are using; you would use the same formula on

---

[23] It's really not. Most radios don't have an easy way to enter MMSI numbers, and the interface for dialing, answering, and acknowledging the answer varies depending on how much the engineer designing the user interface had to drink the night before he built it. Sometimes, it was a lot.

any relevant hailing channel. But there are times when you might want to be explicit in identifying the channel you are calling on:

> *Velcro, Velcro, Velcro,* this is *Serenity, Serenity, Serenity* on channel 13, over.

Although it seems obvious that if someone can hear you they are already tuned in to the right channel, many stations monitor multiple radios simultaneously scanning different channels. Large commercial vessels, for instance, have to maintain a watch on Channel 13 as well as 16 or some alternate VTS channel. If the watchstander isn't staring at the radio bank when your call comes through, it's not necessarily obvious which channel you were calling on.

This is particularly true when you are not on 16, which most people will assume to be the default. And when you clear out on a channel that you will not continue to monitor, it's good practice to mention that also:

> This is *Serenity*, no response heard on 13, *Serenity* will return to channel 16, out.

That way, if the party you were trying to raise on 13 missed you there, they know where to find you later.

Answering a Radio Call

What if you are on the receiving end of being hailed?

If you caught the whole call and know who is calling you, it's simple. After you hear "over," you pick up your own mike and reply:

> *Velcro,* this is *Serenity,* over.

Because they initiated the call, they are running the conversation... you just need to listen for what comes next and answer. If you have been practicing your listening skills as suggested, you shouldn't have any trouble understanding the rest of the conversation. And we already talked about your fallback pro word if you *still* don't quite catch it:

`Velcro, I didn't copy, please say again.`

But sometimes you may not even get quite that far. Perhaps you didn't catch the name of the vessel calling you. That's still no problem because you have a way to identify them—they are the vessel hailing you!

`Vessel hailing Serenity, go ahead, over.`

They should repeat their name when they go ahead, allowing you to copy[24] it on the next round of the conversation. Or, once you've established communication, you can ask them to "say again" their name.

And sometimes, people call you without knowing *your* vessel's name, as in the prior examples. In that case, you might not be completely certain that you are the target. But if no one else answers and you believe that you may be who they are looking for, you should reply:

`Vessel calling the 40-foot white boat in position 46 degrees 15.2 minutes North by 126 degrees 1 minute West, this is the 46-foot Bayliner Serenity, over.`

---

[24] "Copy" is pretty common radio slang... it just means to receive and understand the transmission.

You'll work out between the two of you fairly quickly whether or not you are who they are looking for once you start chatting.

Switch to a Working Channel

Velcro, Serenity. Let's switch to channel 68, over.
Serenity, Velcro, roger 68. Out.

Then you both switch your radios over and continue your conversation. You may go through an abbreviated hailing routine all over again, depending on who you are talking to and how familiar you are with one another, but it's not required.

Clear the Air
Once you have finished your discussion, you should clear the air to make it clear to other users that you no longer need the channel. This is as fast and simple as giving your name and saying "out."

Serenity out.

ABOUT YOUR BOAT NAME _____

It's time to have The Talk about your boat name.

Look, we're not here to judge. It's like naming your kid: very meaningful, very personal, and entirely up to you. We can, for the sake of argument, assume that *Knotty Bouyz* is a name that tugs at your heartstrings, evoking some poignant

memory that sustains and motivates you through your days out on the water. Fine.

But just because it's your baby doesn't mean anyone is going to have the slightest idea what you are saying when you say it over the radio.

Radio is a pretty poor technology for transmitting human speech—you lose certain frequency ranges, introduce static and fuzz in all the wrong places, and get none of the benefits of face-to-face hints and innuendo.

So if you care about people understanding you when it's time to identify your vessel, you should follow some basic rules when you name your boat.

Good boat names should fit five basic criteria. They should be:

- Short
- Have a common, single spelling
- Easily understood on the radio
- Not be ubiquitous
- Personally meaningful

You should also think about how the syllables fit together, understanding that soft schwa sounds are chameleons on the radio, possibly interpreted as many different vowels. The human ear is a wonderful editor when presented with only scraps of sound, but it will default to filling in the most common or likely words for the context... *Bouyz* is probably not in the top ten.

So as much fun as colorfully ambiguous homonyms and creative spelling might be when you are carousing on the dock, understand that you're making your life more difficult when you try to communicate on the radio with such names.

When Your Boat Doesn't Have a Name

Not every boat has a name, and you don't have to name yours if you don't want to. Many kayakers and ski boats have radios on board but no name.

In that case, it's perfectly fine to identify yourself in whatever way will be most easily

understood by your audience. The most common method is to describe the vessel and length:
- 14-foot Yellow Kayak
- White Reinell Ski Boat
- Sailing Dinghy With Red Sail

Whatever is distinctive enough to identify you in that situation and can be used consistently through the conversation is fine—it doesn't even have to be the same as your identifier on the next occasion.

Specialized Protocols

Safety Broadcasts

There is a special category of radio calls that do not fit the general format described earlier. These are broadcasts; a Mayday call is one example, but you'll hopefully never need to make that one. We covered distress calls in the Emergency section because you need to know how to make them, but not all broadcasts are emergencies.

The most common non-emergency broadcast you might hear or make is a Securité (pronounced sec-your-i-tay) call. Securité means what you think it means, and, like Mayday and Pan Pan, is French in origin. Also like those words, it's a pro word, reserved only for this particular use.

A safety broadcast isn't urgent or an emergency, but it helps keep emergencies from developing when used appropriately.

You'll probably hear these fairly regularly wherever you are boating in the United States; the Coast Guard makes regular safety broadcasts to highlight inclement weather conditions or other operations mariners need to be aware of. Commercial traffic may also announce their intentions to prevent incidents from occurring; dive boats or survey vessels that are making unusual maneuvers or that are restricted somehow in their ability to maneuver will usually make a Securité call so nearby vessels won't be surprised when they behave unexpectedly.

You can use safety messages, too, whenever you think it is appropriate. Are you about to inch your way into a blind channel with limited maneuvering room and no idea who is on the other end? Check it out:

Securité, Securité, Securité, this is *Serenity, Serenity, Serenity*, a 46-foot Bayliner entering Dodd Narrows heading northbound. Any concerned or opposing traffic come back on channel 16, *Serenity* out.

Pirate or not, I don't like the little guy's chances here if he hasn't communicated his intentions clearly.

Or say your engine goes out in a shipping channel. There's no one in sight, and you are confident that you know what the issue is and can fix it shortly. There is no urgency here, so you don't need assistance.

All the same, if a ferry is coming around the next headland at twenty knots, it's a good idea to get on their radar (figuratively speaking) well before they come screaming up on you. So before you crack the engine compartment, you get on the horn.

Securité, Securité, Securité, all stations, all stations, all stations. This is *Serenity, Serenity, Serenity.* My position is 47 decimal 580 degrees North by 122 decimal 538 West, in Rich Passage. I am having engine difficulties and am unable to maneuver for approximately one zero minutes. Any concerned traffic, please contact *Serenity* on Channel 16. Out.

And that's it—a common formula that you will want to remember, because many safety and urgency formats follow it:
- Pro word
- Station being called
- Your station
- Your position
- Safety message

In fact, if things get dicey, you are going to turn your Securité call *into* a Pan Pan (urgency) call—you see that ferry bearing down on you, that's urgent!

If there is a particular vessel you want to be sure is getting the message, you can change from "all stations" to the specific vessel name—the ferry, perhaps, that you suspect will be coming around that corner soon.

You can expect a brief acknowledgment in such cases but typically, your Securité broadcasts will be made "in the blind," to no one in particular, and will receive no response. That's okay—it doesn't mean it wasn't heard or that other vessels aren't using the information you provided to stay safe.

You hear people making safety broadcasts in a variety of situations:
- When they are about to transit a narrow passage
- When they encounter a deadhead or other dangerous

obstacle in busy channels
- When they are having maneuverability issues

You simply have to use your own judgment when it comes to making these broadcasts. Again, listening to what others are doing on the radio will be your gold standard for understanding what you should be doing.

Receiving a Safety Broadcast

It should be pretty obvious that you need to pay attention to any Securité messages that you receive while out on the water — they are giving you information you need to stay safe.

Most of the time, it is pretty clear how to handle them and no response is required. Stay clear of boats with diver's down; get out of the path of a cable-laying vessel.

But sometimes, the response is exactly what is requested; the vessel transiting the narrow channel used in the example above, for instance. What if you're already in the channel? Well, they asked for concerned traffic to reply, and you're concerned now... so get in touch!

> Securité, Securité, Securité, this is *Velcro*, *Velcro*, *Velcro*, a 30-foot sailing vessel entering Dodd Narrows heading northbound. Any concerned or opposing traffic come back on channel 16, *Serenity* out.
>
> *Velcro*, this is *Serenity*. We're a 46-foot motor vessel, currently about midway through Dodd Narrows, southbound. Can you delay your transit until we come out down there, over?
>
> *Serenity*, roger that, we'll wait until you

go by, thanks for the heads-up, over.

Of course, conversations will be specific to the message and the situation. But this is exactly what radios, and safety messages, are for! Don't be afraid to reach out if you have concerns or need clarification about the situation.

Emergency Protocols

Although radios are useful for a lot of different reasons, the major underlying reason that most boaters carry them is in case of an emergency.

Almost no one spends much time thinking about what they will actually do if that emergency happens, however.

Like every aspect of radio use, putting a little forethought into making an emergency call can pay big dividends when the time comes. Although it's not hard, there are a few things you will need to know and decisions you will need to make. Mid-catastrophe is not the time you first want to be considering those choices.

Types of Assistance Calls

Everybody knows what a Mayday call is, but there are actually several different options for getting assistance over the radio if you get into trouble out on the water.

Knowing when to make the call, and what call to make, is as vital to emergency radio use as knowing the basic details about turning the radio on and making a transmission. Lives have been lost because the call went out too late; in other cases, incidents were prevented entirely by someone making a quick and mundane sort of call for assistance long before the situation could become urgent.

These calls can be made on the appropriate channels using either VHF or SSB; the format of the transmission is the same either way. Your first choice will depend on the situation. If you are in the middle of a crowded harbor and a fire breaks out, VHF is the easy choice.[25] Thousands of miles offshore, the choice might be different. But don't forget that VHF will quickly reach any vessels that are close by who might assist. If a freighter is just

---

[25] Don't forget non-radio distress signals; in fact, if you are surrounded by other boats, your fastest way to get assistance may just be to step on deck and yell.

over the horizon, it might be more important that they hear your first call rather than a Coast Guard station a thousand miles away.

And EPIRB takes the initial conversation out of your hands entirely. With the push of a button, you'll send your distress call and position automatically. Rescuers will certainly reach out to you over VHF or SSB for more information, though.

There's no penalty for using as many ways as possible to yell for help, either. Choose the best option first, but don't hesitate to repeat your call over as many systems as possible until you reach someone.

Elsewhere in this book, we suggest choosing brevity over formality when making calls; for instance, dropping the repetition of your name or the recipient station name.

> Don't skip any protocol step with any urgency message whatsoever!

The repetition serves an important purpose, and sticking to the internationally agreed-upon message format can help recipients understand your message even if it becomes garbled... something that is always more likely in a stressful situation.

Assistance: Call the Coast Guard Directly

In circumstances where you need help, but there is no urgent or immediate danger (say, you're out of gas, or lost), you can make the least waves by simply hailing the Coast Guard directly on a channel they monitor. You can always raise them on 16; most sectors also guard a working channel, 22A, and you can try them there first to avoid taking up any bandwidth on 16.

Coast Guard Sector San Francisco, Coast

Guard Sector San Francisco,[26] this is *Serenity, Serenity, Serenity* on 22 Alpha, over.

If you don't reach them on 22A, just try it again on 16 (and they'll probably shift you right back to a working channel anyway when you make it clear there is no emergency).

In this sort of situation, the U.S. Coast Guard will typically try to connect you with either a nearby Good Samaritan or a commercial assistance service such as Towboat U.S. Of course, you could also make those calls directly and leave the Coast Guard out of it. But the Coast Guard has big transmitters and can get commercial services on the phone, so they may be better situated to getting help for you.

It's also a good idea to get the Coast Guard involved so that they are in the loop if the situation deteriorates. If no other resources can get to you or if things start to go from bad to worse, it's faster for the Coast Guard to get their own assets involved if they already know where you are and what is happening.

Urgency: Pan Pan

The international pro word indicating an urgent safety situation, which does *not* involve imminent danger to vessel or crew, is *Pan Pan*. Some folks pronounce it like frying "pan," and others use a pronunciation more like "pawn"— [27]either way, the

---

[26] You can always just hail "Coast Guard" almost anywhere in the world and the closest station will answer. It's good to be specific if possible, however; for instance, in the Strait of Georgia along the U.S./Canadian border, you're likely to end up talking to the U.S. Coast Guard even if you're in Canadian waters... not very useful.

[27] My French ain't great, but the ITU claims it should be pronounced like the French word "panne" (meaning, appropriately, "breakdown"). When I hear someone French say it, it sounds like pan in frying pan to me, but you will hear people argue (when drunk, and nothing better to occupy themselves with) that "pawn" is correct. If you need to use it, don't sweat the difference, just try to get it in the ballpark.

repetition ensures that people will know what you mean.

Many situations where Mayday calls are used could be better handled with a Pan Pan. For example:

```
Pan Pan, Pan Pan, Pan Pan. All stations,
all stations, all stations. This is
Serenity, Serenity, Serenity. My position
is 34 decimal 205 degrees North by 120
decimal 661 degrees West and my course is
145 degrees True, making 8 knots. I have a
crew member on board who has sustained a
broken leg. I'm requesting assistance from
any vessel in the vicinity who can provide
medical or evacuation assistance, over.
```

Because there is no imminent danger to life or of losing the vessel, this is a step down on the urgency scale. You will still get a very rapid response from the Coast Guard or other rescue agencies, but because the situation is more controlled and less dangerous, they can scale their response accordingly.

Distress: Mayday

Putting out a Mayday call is a big deal, and it shouldn't be done lightly. Mayday shuts down the air and starts the wheels turning at rescue coordination centers and bases all through the region. Ships at sea may be diverted; aircraft can be launched; rescuers will suit up and get ready to put themselves in harm's way on your behalf.

Obviously, all this should only happen in the event that you are in real danger. There's no threshold for this; no one makes that decision but you.[28] The Coast Guard will not second-guess a Mayday call that isn't a prank (and, at least initially, all pranks are taken seriously as well), even in the most apparently benign conditions. In fact, there are many circumstances in which they will evacuate boaters even in the event the boaters themselves decide they are no longer in imminent danger.

Mayday calls must be made on the international hailing and distress frequency, which corresponds to Channel 16 for your VHF; many newer radios have a big, fat, red button that will automatically switch your radio to that channel and to high power mode for just this purpose.

The call format is important, and you should follow it as closely as possible; it has six essential blocks of information, all delivered in order and in one transmission:

The call	Mayday, Mayday, Mayday. This is *Serenity, Serenity, Serenity.* Mayday *Serenity.*

---

[28] There is an official definition put forth by the IMO, however: when a ship or person "...is threatened by grave and imminent danger and requires immediate assistance." All terms in the definition are subject to personal interpretation, of course.

Your position	Our position is 34 decimal 205 degrees North by 120 decimal 661 degrees West; Point Conception bears zero three seven degrees true at two-zero miles.
Nature of distress	We have a fire on board.
Assistance required	We need to be evacuated.
Number of persons on board	There are four souls on board.
Other information	*Serenity* is a 34-foot sailboat, white decks, blue hull. The sails are down and we are not making way. We have one person injured but able to move. Over.

This particular order of information is important—it's designed so that the most critical information goes first. If all you can manage to do is get out your position, rest assured someone will come looking for you, even if they don't know the exact problem. If you start off instead just yelling about a fire, however, and then the radio goes dead before you get around to saying where you are at, no one knows where to send help.

A position by latitude and longitude is preferred, but any information that will definitively establish your location is acceptable. If you have time, it's good to either repeat this information or provide multiple references, as in the example—there is nothing more important about the call than ensuring rescuers can find you.

This extends to providing information about your course and speed if you are still making way.

Other information can include any sort of detail that will help rescuers decide what to send and by what method.

The Coast Guard will reply and slowly take you through the longest checklist in the world[29] that will revisit much of the information you have already provided them.

DSC Distress Calls

Digital Selective Calling dramatically reduces the complexity of making a distress call.

DSC distress calls are always treated as a Mayday, but some units allow a pre-coded type of distress to be included with the digital message. These include:
- Fire or explosion
- Grounding
- Man overboard
- Collision
- Sinking
- Disabled and adrift

You may not have time to key this information in— recreational transceivers are notoriously difficult to enter data on —and most radios have a simple one-button distress feature that will transmit a general distress call.

---

[29] It's not really that long. But it will feel like it when you are sinking.

Emergency Protocols - 73

If the radio has a dedicated GPS receiver or is attached to an external GPS unit, it will also automatically send your current position along with the time.

The acknowledgment is another electronic chirp on the control channel that tells your radio that a coast station has received your message. Your radio will automatically retune itself to the proper distress frequency, and you should complete the transmission as outlined in the grid above—the only difference being that you should include your MMSI number as your station identifier (instead of or in addition to your vessel name).

This duplicates information that has probably already been sent, but the redundancy is valuable. And if you can't get around to sending it again, at least someone knows where you are and that you need help.

DSC is fast and accurate, making it by far the best method to transmit a distress call. If properly wired up, you can hit the button and get back to dealing with the emergency, knowing that your vessel name and position have been put out over the air. If you have time to complete the call, that's great, but often there is no time; in recent tests conducted by Boat U.S.,[30] it was found that in a typical small craft fire, you have only three or four minutes from discovering the flames to being in the water. Listen to a conventional distress call from another vessel the next time you get a chance—the conversation with the Coast Guard can easily consume a full minute. That's a minute that you aren't donning a life jacket or fighting a fire or plugging a leak.

DSC can also be used to transmit urgency and safety (Pan Pan and Securité) calls. The process is similar to making a distress call, although without the ease of one-button operation. Each radio is different, but typically you will have to maneuver your way through a series of menus to set up the call properly. One sign that you are not, in fact, in an emergency situation is that you will have plenty of time to do that.

---

[30] http://www.boatus.com/magazine/2017/boat-burn-tests.asp

When To Make The Call

The hardest part of any of these calls is making the decision on when and what sort of aid to request.

There's always Monday morning quarterbacking after an emergency. One thing you can be sure of is that you will make some bad decisions along the way; you'll definitely screw some things up, and some of those might be your radio communications. Many more Maydays are broadcast than there are actual emergencies. People panic or put themselves into unwise situations that they didn't have to be in and wind up calling for aid they might not really need.

There is debate, from time to time, about boaters relying on the radio as Plan A in case their trip goes bad, instead of preparing and equipping themselves properly for the voyage. In fact, nearly every time an expensive offshore rescue is undertaken, armchair sailors come out of the woodwork to chronicle the deficiencies of the boaters in trouble and argue that the situation wasn't truly worthy of a distress call. And in fact, even some sailors who have made distress calls question later whether or not it was the appropriate action to take.

But within the Coast Guard and other emergency services, there is no debate.

Better than anyone, the Coast Guard understands the increasing amount of danger that you put everyone in when you contact them only *after* everything has already gone from bad to worse. What could have been a simple, if embarrassing, tow back to the marina in the mid-afternoon with storm clouds on the horizon can turn into a dangerous helicopter rescue in pitch black conditions and 30-knot winds if you delay asking for assistance for too long.

So it's important to know your options for assistance calls and to be comfortable making a less urgent one *before* the situation escalates to the point where you might need to make a Mayday call.

Nothing can really answer this question other than

experience. But it's exactly the kind of experience you don't want to have. Most people, fortunately, never have to make a distress call through the entire course of their boating career, let alone so many that they can really learn from them.

If the moment comes, you will probably just have to rely on common sense and seamanship to make your decision.

One rule of thumb is to make a call as soon as you think about it. Situations tend to escalate faster than our ability to process them; when you start thinking you may be in trouble, you probably **are** in trouble. And now that you know there are options less intense than a full Mayday call, you can exercise one of them without fear of overreacting. Getting the Coast Guard in the loop will mean bringing professionals into the decision-making process—cooler heads will be able to assess your situation and help you get it under control or dispatch the appropriate types of assistance.

Receiving an Assistance Call

And what should you do if you *receive* one of these messages from another vessel?

For most mariners, most of the time, you probably won't have to do anything. If you keep a log, it's prudent to log both the time and content of the message (particularly any location and identification, if received)... see the Logging sidebar for reasons why.

As a radio user, you *do* have some responsibilities during a distress call—namely, shutting up and staying off the air. It may be obvious that you must do this during the initial transmissions, but the responsibility can extend as long as the Mayday vessel or the Coast Guard sees fit.

This is indicated by a pro word "Seelonce Mayday." When this is transmitted, it indicates that *only emergency traffic* may be transmitted on that channel. Were you trying to arrange to meet your fishing buddy at a common anchorage for the night? Too bad! You have to wait until you hear "Seelonce Feenee," the pro word that ends the radio silence.[31]

There is also the very rarely used "Prudonce" or "Seelonce Prudonce" which allows *limited* use of the channel by other vessels—quick transmissions that do not interfere with the distress traffic. None of the restrictions apply to any vessel actively involved in the distress call.

Responding to a Distress Call

But there are circumstances in which you must make a reply and take action to render assistance if you receive a Mayday call.

It's long been a custom of the sea that mariners will make the utmost effort, consistent with prudent seamanship and their own safety, to rescue others in distress. In 1982, the United Nations Convention on the Law of the Sea (UNCLOS) was amended to mandate that signatories *require* vessels flying under their flag render assistance to those in distress at sea.

The United States implemented this in 46 U.S. Code § 2304, which imposes possible fines of up to $1,000 and 2 years imprisonment for any master of a U.S. flagged vessel failing to respond to any individual in danger of being lost at sea. Other laws, both state and federal, provide Good Samaritan protection from liability in such cases.

> Your first duty under this provision is to ensure that a distress message you have received is transmitted to the proper authorities.

For any coastal boater, this is nearly automatic and out of your hands—the Coast Guard has better radios, taller antennas, and professional watchstanders. They almost always hear what you

---

[31] What's up with the screwy words? Well, they are bastardized French, just like Mayday, chosen because they are unique, come through static well, and are understandable to international listeners.

hear, only better. You should hear their reply almost immediately, and your obligation in that respect is discharged.

But what if the Coast Guard doesn't reply? What if there is no other reply? What if the distress signal was visual—a flare or flags, that only you are in a position to see?

The Coast Guard recommends you wait three to five minutes to allow them a chance to reply if they have heard any radio message. If they do not, you must attempt to convey the message to them yourself, using a Mayday Relay call.[32]

Making a Mayday Relay Call

First, acknowledge receipt of the message (in this scenario, *Velcro* is the vessel in distress; you are aboard *Serenity*, and have heard their call, and noted that the Coast Guard has not replied):

Mayday, *Velcro*, *Velcro*, *Velcro*.[33] This is *Serenity*, *Serenity*, *Serenity*. Received Mayday, over.

If the other vessel hears you and replies, you can take that opportunity to get the additional information from them you will need to pass on to the Coast Guard (the same information found in the Mayday grid above). If they don't, you will have to fill in the blanks from what you have seen or heard. It's best not to guess—stick to things you are sure about, like your own position, the strength of the signal, and so on.

If you are equipped with DSC, there is a distress relay call format. However, on many radios, this requires a considerable amount of manual input (unlike the one-button Distress call you can use if your own vessel is in trouble). In many cases, it may be

---

[32] You may hear the Coast Guard itself use this format to rebroadcast Maydays when other boats are in trouble.

[33] Note that for a Mayday received via DSC, you may use the Mayday vessel's MMSI number instead of the name.

faster and easier to make the relay call manually, just as if you do not have DSC.

> Mayday Relay, Mayday Relay, Mayday Relay. This is *Serenity, Serenity, Serenity.* Mayday. *Serenity* received a Mayday call from the motor vessel *Velcro* at 1432 Pacific Daylight Time. *Velcro's* reported position at that time was just west of Blind Island in Blind Bay off Shaw Island. *Velcro* has struck a rock and is taking on water and requests pumps or evacuation. *Velcro* reports 3 souls on board. Mayday Relay, over.

The Coast Guard may direct you to stand by or render other assistance. Part of that assistance, in the event the other vessel is unable to establish direct communication, might be continuing to serve as a relay.

This is radio work of the highest value and greatest difficulty. All your skills will be tested as you must remain calm and clear to coordinate between multiple stations (likely not only the Coast Guard sector and distress vessel but also other Good Samaritan vessels and incoming rescue craft).

Although it will be stressful, the best way to manage will be to double down on everything you've learned here and been practicing:

- **Keep a log** — Although jotting notes down might seem like a waste of time in an emergency, it will serve two important purposes:
    - Logging will force you to slow down; it may seem maddening, but accuracy and clarity will both benefit.

- Important information will be preserved and available for rapid reference even if the original source goes off the air, e.g., contact is lost with the distress vessel.
- **Compose your sentence before you transmit it** — Think through what you want to say, then read it out like a script. You can even compose, briefly, in your log, if it helps.
- **Mind your boat** — It's easy to get absorbed in radio traffic and lose sight of the fact you have your own vessel to worry about. The last thing you need is to end up in your own emergency situation.

As to whether or not you must directly assist the vessel in distress, the law is murkier. The key element of § 2304 reads, "… so far as the master or individual in charge can do so without serious danger to the master's or individual's vessel or individuals on board."

So, in practice, almost no court will question your decision not to intervene except in the most egregious cases.

It will always be a question of your judgment of capabilities and moral obligation, as has ever been the case on the high seas.

SAR SYSTEM

Just as with knowing how your radio works and what the protocol is when you need to call for help, it can be useful to understand what exactly is happening on the other end of that transmission when the authorities get the call.

The responsibility for responding to distress calls is, at the global level, governed by the International Convention on Maritime Search and Rescue. Much of this is implemented—and many of your radio features and capabilities have been driven by —the Global Maritime Distress and Safety System established by the convention.

IMO splits the oceans into 13 regions and assigns adjacent countries responsibility for coordinating rescue activities in those regions.

Most countries handle this by establishing a series of Rescue Coordination Centers (RCCs), which field distress reports and coordinate various agencies that may respond. The RCCs don't directly receive radio distress calls, but they do get initial reports of EPIRB activation from the COSPAS-SARSAT satellite network.

Radio distress calls are fielded by local operations, such as Coast Guard Groups and Sectors. In the United States, these watchstanders monitor the National Distress System (NDS), a network of around 300 VHF transceivers and high-sites[34], as well as sites from the new Rescue 21 system, which incorporate DSC and advanced direction-finding capabilities as well as closing coverage gaps in the NDS. There are around 88 of those gaps, nationwide, so the difference is not trivial.

Additionally, the Coast Guard maintains two Communications Area Master Stations, one each for the Atlantic and Pacific, to monitor HF (High Frequency, or SSB channels) distress and hailing frequencies from five remote antenna sites. Communication Station Kodiak also guards HF and VHF independently.

Coast Guard watchstanders are well-practiced at handling distress calls received either directly or via relay. You will hear them run down the same checklist of information for every call. Although the radio operator will stay in contact with the vessel in distress, in the background, that information is being passed along to the relevant RCC.

The RCC doesn't usually directly control any rescue assets but can task a response to a variety of agencies with different capabilities. Depending on the nature and location of the vessel in distress, they can send anything from an Air Force C-130 with pararescue jumpers to a local fire department dinghy to the scene. The RCCs also have AMVER on tap, the Automated Mutual-Assistance Vessel Rescue System, a voluntary reporting system by commercial vessels which allows coordinators to find

---

[34] These are, literally, simply high points such as mountains where a radio repeater has been located for better coverage. You may hear them referred to on the air or in informational posts as as the "Mount Such-and-such high site" from time to time.

the closest civilian ship and relay requests for assistance. Frequently, on high seas rescues, AMVER ships are in the best position to respond. More than 2,800 mariners have been saved by AMVER vessels since 2000.

The RCC will continue working the incident until the vessel is safe, the crew has been rescued, or contact is lost and all hope of survival is gone.

Local incidents may never be escalated to the RCC, at least in the United States. Other countries have different processes, but the general procedures remain similar. It's not uncommon for an RCC from one country to request assets from another country that is either better positioned or equipped to address the emergency.[35]

---

[35] So if, as in the scenario in the last section where you hailed the U.S. Coast Guard from Canadian waters, you would in fact still receive assistance... we were just trying to scare you a little.

Using Radio in the Real World

By now, you've been following along long enough to notice that most of the radio traffic you hear from day to day doesn't exactly match the protocols you read about earlier.

Some of this is due to sloppy usage and amateur operators. But we have a dirty secret that we can now reveal to you: some of it is simply because protocol is only a starting point. Many of the conversations you overhear only adopt the aspects of proper protocol that are *necessary in that moment* for the operators to understand one another. A blind and slavish adherence to protocol can be as bad as ignoring it entirely.[36]

Remember, the two most important points of radio use are:
- Brevity
- Clarity

If you can achieve those objectives in practice *without* completely adhering to the protocol, then go ahead and do it!

Don't think of the time you spent reading about protocol as being wasted, though. This is a scenario where you have to know the rules in order to break them. Not every protocol is optional in every situation. If you don't have a solid footing to understand why or why not you should be using them, you're in no position to judge when you can skip or modify those protocols.

But now that you have at least a rudimentary grasp of proper radio protocol, you're ready to start making some of your own judgments about how to use it. In this chapter, we'll talk about radio *practice*, in both senses of the word:

Practice ~

1. The actual application or use of an idea, belief, or method as opposed to theories about such application

---

[36] Well, maybe not *as* bad. But bad!

or use.

2. Repeated exercise in or performance of an activity or skill so as to acquire or maintain proficiency in it.

So we'll show you the reality of how professional users make and receive radio calls as well as showing you some techniques for talking on the radio more comfortably and naturally yourself.

Rehearsal

The reality is that most people aren't good at talking on the radio because they don't get the opportunity to practice it often. If you're the typical recreational boater, you're probably only out on the water a handful of weekends and—if you're lucky—a single good week during an average season.

And those days and hours are usually when the weather is best and the opportunities for radio-required interactions the fewest.

So you have no reason to feel bad about not being comfortable on the radio right away. Like any skill, it's one that takes practice.

Think It Through Ahead of Time

In many respects, talking on the radio is exactly as simple as it looks—just punch the key and spit it out. Overthinking this process leads to a lot of the trouble that people have with their radios!

In some ways, radio makes talking *easier*, not harder.

You get to say pretty much what you want, you get to think about it before you say it, and no one can interrupt! You don't have to get the whole conversation out in one shot, either; you get to take breaks in the middle and think about what you are saying.

In fact, it might be those pauses that screw us up so much! Usually, we get to talk without thinking about it too much. When you add a step to the process, it's bound to throw us off. To balance that extra complication, it's best to keep sentences simple and to the point.

Don't be afraid to take your time. Even though getting your call out succinctly is part of being a good radio user, it will always be faster if you don't bungle it and have to repeat yourself.

Slow down enough to make sure you are using good (if not always complete) protocol and procedure, and that other stations can understand what you are saying.

Let's deconstruct the process a little more before you get started.

It's Not a Phone Call, But Let's Talk About Phone Calls For a Minute

Most of your experience of talking into small hand-held devices probably comes from your phone, and that's not a bad place to start with thinking about how to use the radio.

Think about how you chat with someone on the phone. You probably speak normally, conversationally, like they were in the same room, but maybe not looking at you—body language is lost, your words have to make up for it a little bit. Otherwise, it doesn't feel strange at all, does it?

The major difference with radio use is that the one-way nature of a transmission takes away some of the casual affect of a conversation. There's nowhere to insert the little conversational lubricants that most of us use: the "uh-huh," "yeah," "right… right…," "okay," and so on that you scatter in between statements to let the other party know that you're still on the same page.

And they can't just pipe up to move the conversation along if you start to stumble, either. When you have the mike button depressed, you are carrying the whole burden of keeping the thread alive. On the phone, if you hit a rough patch getting your point across, the other party can interject with a clarification or question to help you… not so on the radio! If you get a sentence started without knowing quite where it's going to end up, you're going to feel awkward and alone pretty fast.

Connections may not be as clear, either. Radio doesn't pick up on the total range of sound that you produce. So your tone of voice may not come across clearly; your meaning will be carried in the words alone. And static can interfere even with those, either erasing them entirely or rendering them ambiguous.

So radio use *has* to be slightly more formal… but only slightly.

It's Not Like The Movies, Either

Many novices mistake what they see in the movies or on TV for the reality of radio use, but most movies make a hash of it. They are overloaded with jargon and unrealistic conversations.[37] If you model your own use on what you see there, you're going to come across as being pretty weird. "Ten-four, roger, good buddy, over and out," is a transmission you will only ever hear from a complete neophyte.

In reality, you won't need to know a lot of jargon. In fact, plain English is becoming increasingly preferred even on military and police radio nets. It turns out, unsurprisingly, that what we understand most easily under stress are the same basic speech patterns that we use normally every day.

There are some times that Hollywood gets it right, though, and you can check out those films or shows for some cues.

Movies and TV shows that get radio mostly right

- End of Watch
- Generation Kill (HBO Series)
- Platoon
- The Wire (HBO Series)
- Happy Valley (BBC; sure, they talk funny, but the procedure is good)
- Cops (obviously; much of the radio traffic is edited, however)

---

[37] Which is fine! They're telling a story, not putting together an instruction manual for radio use.

Getting Tone and Volume Correct

For technical reasons that you will be happy we aren't going to go into, radio doesn't carry the full range of tones that your voice produces. In general, lower tones will not carry as well over VHF. Particularly for men, it may be important to pitch your voice higher than in typical conversations in order to make yourself understood. And the kind of varying intonation you might use for in-person or even phone conversations for emphasis or extra meaning will likely be lost in a radio transmission.[38]

Part of the problem in determining the proper tone and level of voice is that none of us know what we really sound like, even in person. If you've ever heard a recording of yourself speaking, you know that your voice sounds different to others than it does in your head. The vibration of your voice through your skull happens at a lower frequency, making your voice sound deeper to yourself than it does to everyone else. So you already know that how you hear yourself is an imperfect guide for adjusting your speech.

Of course, you can just record yourself talking if you want to hear what you sound like in person, but there's no easy way to record yourself talking on the radio.

> One great way to hear what you sound like on the radio is to take advantage of any automated radio check systems that may serve your region.

SeaTow has an automated radio check system set up on a handful of frequencies with stations scattered throughout the

---

[38] This is so common in English that you probably don't realize you are using it every day, but think about the different ways you might pronounce the word "really" to vary the meaning... a very high pitch to express skepticism, flat for emphasis, a falling tone for sarcasm. Those subtleties will largely be lost in a radio transmission.

United States.[39] Repeaters listen for your transmission and then play it back to you over the air so you can get a sense of your transmission strength and clarity.

You shouldn't hog the channel, but there's nothing to stop you from using it judiciously to get a feel for what it sounds like on the other end of the call. You can try holding the mike at different distances or locations from your mouth and see what difference it makes; speak louder or softer, until you dial in something that feels natural and sounds good.

Some tips to help make your pronunciation clear: Make your consonant letters flat and distinct; these tend to blur together. Vowels may be exaggerated slightly.[40]

Practice Your Performance

Like any performance, your radio production will be made great by the time you spend in rehearsal.

Because it's so important, and because you have the time to do so (remember, you control the conversation! There's no need to transmit before you're ready to do so), you should rehearse to yourself, briefly, what you plan to say on the radio every time before you key the microphone.

While that's part of the essence of every transmission, it's also just a short conceptual leap away from a technique that will have you mastering radio use in no time. And that is to be rehearsing radio calls in your head *constantly*, not just when you are definitely going to make a call.

Building scenarios in your head about what your next steps

---

[39] You can find a map with the stations and the proper procedure to follow on the SeaTow website here:
https://www.seatow.com/tools-and-education/automated-radio-check

[40] You can get an idea of how this sounds by consulting the section under Advanced Radio Techniques discussing how numbers should be pronounced.

are going to be when you are out running a boat is part of the mental mindset of every competent skipper. You see a squall brewing on the horizon; you start thinking about the process of shortening sail. You see a cruise ship heave into view on a constant bearing; you think about altering your course. You visualize your route, consider other obstacles and conditions, imagine the motions you will go through to effect the changes. Then you do it!

Such little internal conversations are a constant part of boating. And all you need to do to continually improve your radio performance is to start to incorporate radio conversations into those visualizations.

The cruise ship scenario is an easy one. Obviously, you imagine calling them directly to determine their course and intentions, thinking about how you would phrase it, what they might reply, how you would conclude the conversation.

But let's talk about the squall for a second. A lot of boating scenarios don't necessarily or naturally involve a radio call… or you'd already be thinking about it more! But they might. Say a crew person is swept overboard during the sail change. Or you shred the sails, the engine won't start, you're getting blown toward a reef. If you spend much time reading marine accident reports[41], there's no shortage of chains of events that start with relatively innocuous decisions that could lead to a rapid need for a radio call.

So tack those scenarios into your regular rehearsals of ordinary maneuvers. Imagine making a Pan Pan call for a COB; think about calling Towboat U.S. when your engine won't start.

It only takes seconds in your head, but they add up. At first, you may feel silly doing this (relax, it's not out loud—no one needs to know!), but with repeated internal dialogs of this sort, you'll be getting something similar to the experience you would actually get making the real calls. Soon, it will feel smooth and natural to plan out what you are saying before you say it…

---

[41] You don't? It's just me? Oh.

because you're already doing it regularly. At some point, you won't even consciously have to include that step in your thought process. You'll just do it automatically.

Practicing In Person

One interesting way to practice talking on the radio is to actually do so, but while you are within visual range of the recipient. Standing on the deck of two boats in a common anchorage may be close enough to see one another, but not to easily converse without radio.

But you may find that simply being able to see the other person loosens your tongue considerably and makes it easier to get sentences out.[42] Because you can see the other person, you have all of the same visual cues to conversation that you would if you were speaking in-person. This allows you to forget about the hard parts of losing that aspect of communication and to concentrate primarily on getting your habits of operating in a simplex channel down.

Because VHF isn't appropriate for random chit-chat, you might try this instead with FRS, [43]which does not have any such restrictions and has the perfect range for it.

Performance Anxiety

A lot of radio problems are basically performance anxiety. And not without reason: you're going on air, live, in front of potentially hundreds of people! That puts you on the spot if you're not

---

[42] I stumbled on this technique almost by accident, when I was in college working as a security officer at a mall. The mall had several large parking structures located near one another. When another officer and myself needed to chat but were in different garages, we would naturally gravitate to the common facing sides and have our conversation—but use our walky-talkies instead of trying to yell back and forth. It proved an easy way to become comfortable with using the radio, since I had the visual cues common to in-person conversation, and only had to focus on the back and forth nature of simplex transmission.

[43] If you're not familiar with FRS, or Family Radio Service, we'll talk about it a bit later in the book when we cover other types of radio beyond VHF.

someone who enjoys speaking in front of crowds.

Try using some of the same techniques that people are taught for becoming more comfortable with public speaking:[44]

- Use relaxation techniques such as deep breathing to calm yourself
- Pretend you are an actor delivering a speech on stage; it's not really *you*, it's your character, who is bold, clear, and totally not nervous
- Pretend you are speaking directly to a friend

There's one more unique thing you can tell yourself to help stay calm when you're nervous about screwing up on the radio: no one is going to recognize you in the bar later.

Scripting the Conversation

Sometimes it's a good idea to jot down the basics of what you are going to say before you start talking in order to have that visual prompt in front of you. This may be as far as you can take that technique in some cases, since a two-way conversation where only one party has the script is inevitably going to drift.

But there are other scenarios you might run into frequently where you are basically going to be making the same transmission no matter what. Securité calls are one of these—you are making a general broadcast, probably won't receive any replies, and you know well ahead of time what you need to say. In most cases, they will vary by only a few words.

Write all that out and stick it by the radio! When the time comes to transmit, all you have to do is push the mike button and

---

[44] Glossophobia is the term for the fear of public speaking; you can look up common approaches to treating it (and some of those techniques mirror what you're being taught by this book) but, like seasickness, there's no universal cure... you'll have to figure out what works for you on an individual basis.

read it off a card.[45]

This is also a commonly recommended technique for Mayday transmissions. Many boats have a basic script taped up by the radio. This both ensures that anyone on board can make a distress call in the event the regular radio operator is the one in distress, and it helps you focus on getting it right during the stress of an emergency situation.

You might write up basic scripts for situations like:
- Emergencies
- Making passing arrangements with other boats
- Calling marinas to ask about slip availability for the evening

You can find a set of basic scripts in the Appendix: Basic Scripts.

Of course, eventually, you'll be able to skip most or all of these steps... you'll simply do it all automatically, just like having a regular conversation. Until then, keep rehearsing before you speak!

Dealing with Interruptions

In the real world, not everything goes right! In reality, you'll find that sometimes you get stepped on,[46] or (let's be fair here, either of you could be at fault!) step on someone else's transmission.

Although this is bad form, it happens regularly. Sometimes, due to the vagaries of transmission and reception, you or someone else may be unable to hear the other party talking but

---

[45] Three by five notecards, fast fading into obscurity with the onset of digital note-taking applications, are perfect for this—they enforce brevity and are easy to tack up around the radio for fast reference.
Or you could just use your iPhone, like everybody else.

[46] Cool radio slang for having your transmission interfered with—use it at parties and you won't be able to fight off all the attention.

are sending with enough power to disrupt their transmission. Of course, if you are the one doing the interrupting in such cases, you'll never know it.

But you'll hear it if it's happening while you are trying to listen to the station you're talking to.

There's little point in admonishing anyone about anything over the radio—such disagreements just end up causing more of the same problems they are trying to solve, tying up the air and leading to miscommunication. So resist the urge to yell at the station causing the problems—as noted above, they may not even realize it is happening.

The quickest way to resolve the issue is simply to hop frequencies to a different working channel. As soon as both the conflicting vessels are off the air, jump in immediately to call the boat you were talking to:

Velcro, you were stepped on, let's go up to 72, over.

Then switch up to the new channel and carry on!

This won't work in every situation, however. Notably, if you're trying to raise someone on 16, you don't really have another channel to try for them on—that is the only option.

In these cases, it's best to just back off for a few minutes and let the interrupting boat get their own business concluded. If you have an urgent situation, you should be using the appropriate pro words, and the other boat should respect them (and if they don't, the Coast Guard, with their big, bad, shore-based transmitters that can stomp on just about any vessel's signal, is likely to step in and deal with the matter); otherwise, it's not a big deal to hang back a little bit and take care of your own radio business without interference.

It's also entirely possible—even likely—that you just won't understand what is said at some point. Until you get a lot of hours under your belt, your ear just won't naturally pick up the strangeness of voices on the radio. Even when you are all dialed in, there is always interference, or even folks on the other end of the line who just aren't very good at talking on the radio themselves (buy them a copy of this book!). So get used to saying:

```
Velcro, I didn't copy that, can you say
again, please? Over.
```

WHAT IF YOU MAKE A MAYDAY GOOF?

You'll hear it happen several times in any given cruising season—the high tones of a DSC distress alert call, followed by relay information from the Coast Guard announcing that it has received a Mayday call from some random MMSI number and requesting that any mariners with further information about the vessel please contact them. And, often as not, within a half-hour or so, you'll hear the Coast Guard back on the air: the Mayday was canceled, someone just hit the button on accident.

Someday, that someone could be you!

There's no need to be ashamed, though. Don't go bury your head under your pillow and pretend it didn't happen. The seamanlike way to handle such incidents is to own up to them and cancel them before the relay even happens.

- **Stop transmitting the signal** — Most radios keep sending the DSC call until they receive an acknowledgement. You don't need the acknowledgment, you just want the alert to stop—turning off your radio is one sure way to make that happen.
    - **Turn your radio off** — Leave it off for a few seconds.
- **Turn the radio back on and switch over to the distress frequency** — On VHF, this will be Channel 16; on an SSB, buckle up, because it could be any one (or several) of six different frequencies. You need to give an all-clear on each of them!
- **Key the mike and say:**

```
All stations, all stations, all stations. This
is Serenity, Serenity, Serenity, MMSI number 123
123456. Cancel the distress alert of 1742 sent by
this station. I repeat, cancel the distress alert
sent at 1742 by this station. There is no
emergency, the call was accidental. Serenity out.
```

Do *not* say "cancel Mayday." Mayday *is still a pro word*, even if the first time around was an accident. If your transmission only comes through partially, people will still think you're in trouble out there if they hear that word. If, for some reason, you sent out a Pan Pan, then use the phrase "cancel urgency message of" instead of "cancel the distress alert."

That's it! The Coast Guard is probably going to want to have a discussion with you, but mistakes happen. It will be understood, and you will have handled it in a cool and professional manner.

Standing Watch

Radio watchkeeping is the general term of art for keeping your radio on a specific channel and paying attention to it. This can be as formal or informal as standing any other sort of watch, whether at anchor or underway, but there are legal requirements that may apply, and you should know what they are.

Although widely flouted, FCC 47 CFR §§ 80.148 and 80.310 mandate that any vessel equipped with a "radiotelephone" (these codes were drafted a few years ago) must maintain a standby watch on channel 16 when the radio is not otherwise being used for communication. This is also referred to as "guarding" the channel, which implies a certain degree of vigilance.

This is all part of a general scheme of radio use that makes users responsible for one another, establishing a network of coverage that could never be duplicated by dedicated shore stations or official agencies at any reasonable cost. By participating in the scheme, you are effectively a relay for any other nearby vessel that gets into trouble; conversely, they will also be available to relay or even assist you directly should misfortune befall your own boat.

Apart from the safety aspects of watchkeeping, there is an aspect of prudent seamanship to it. Knowing what is going on around you is part of responsible navigation and vessel operation. By keeping your radio on and tuned to the right channels, you won't miss relevant Securité messages, calls to coordinate passing arrangements, or someone letting you know that your dinghy painter just parted.

Like any other aspect of radio use, solid watchkeeping skills come with practice. You will have to train your ear to pay attention to the radio traffic without being distracted by it.[47] You

---

[47] As a sleep-starved rent-a-cop in college, I learned like many others on graveyard shift how to pull over in a dark alley to catnap while the radio babbled on beside me. I could sleep like a baby through unrelated traffic but as soon as my callsign came over the air, I'd be wide awake.

will learn, over time, to pick out the relevant transmissions and to let the rest fade into the background.

Radio Nets

Local knowledge is as important in radio use as it is in navigation. Knowing what channels are commonly used and what the local lingo is can take you a long way toward sounding like you know what you're doing.

A great way to do this and build your confidence at the same time is to listen to (or participate in) organized radio nets.

A radio net is simply a gathering of operators on a certain channel at a certain time. They are often organized around a specific region or topic; for instance, there are nets dedicated to cruising the Sea of Cortez and others that are composed mostly of people in the middle of a Pacific crossing.

Because you can't just have a load of people transmitting willy-nilly on these frequencies, nets are usually organized to some degree. This can be as basic as having a station acting as a net controller, who serves as a referee and turns the air over to each participating station in turn, or as formal as having a fixed reporting format that each boat must follow. Most nets will offer such instructions as part of their opening at the appointed hour, read out by the net controller. These days, with growing internet access, you can often find such information on dedicated web pages for some of the larger nets.[48]

Nets often have a strong informational component—most include some variety of weather forecasts or reporting, and some are even dedicated to weather forecasts—and some are strongly safety-oriented. These provide a venue for vessels on long or distant passages to check in regularly and serve as a way for the authorities to be alerted if someone fails to reach their destination or report in as expected.

---

[48] See, for example, the British Columbia Boater's Network at https://www.bcbn.ca/

They are also a social forum. People stay in touch across thousands of miles, and with friends they may not have seen in person for years. Nets are part of the cruising community. That means they're a great snapshot of current radio use practice and valuable things to monitor to tune your ear to how it's done.

Most radio nets are on ham or marine SSB frequencies, but some popular anchorages have VHF nets. These serve as a local party line for cruisers in the area and can carry traffic ranging from complaints about speeding dinghies to an online auction for spare fenders.

LOGGING

It's pretty rare for most boat owners today to keep a real, old-fashioned logbook, and even more rare to maintain a radio log. If you hold an RROP you must be able to keep at least a rough written log. But even if you aren't licensed, keeping a radio log can be practical as well as traditional, and it's something to consider if you really want to come across like a radio pro.

Like a regular vessel log, a radio log is a great memory prompt for when and what particular things happened in your conversations. Because you are writing them down in or near the moment itself, your entries are likely to be more accurate than your memories. This is often of particular importance when the conversation involves something detailed, such as position coordinates or rendezvous times.

You also don't always know exactly what might be important in a conversation until much later… by which time that bit may be forgotten if you didn't write it down. Occasionally, the Coast Guard will broadcast a request for information on the last time a particular vessel has been seen or heard from as part of a search operation. It's maddening to realize that you spoke with them a few days ago but can't recall exactly when or where, when their lives might be hanging on that information.

You can keep radio calls logged in your regular vessel log, of course.

- Write down the time of the call
- Include the name of the other station(s) involved
- Summarize the substance of the conversation

If you're entering this inline in your regular log, you get your position information for free—you'll be pretty close to the next closest logged position.[49]

You might also note exceptional characteristics of the transmission itself, such as particularly poor signal strength. This can allow you to spot trends, which in turn can help you troubleshoot your radio system or improve your knowledge of how terrain, position, or conditions affect your reception quality. Some boaters also log distress calls, which can also prove important later on—if the Coast Guard does not get a good location from their radio direction finding (RDF) apparatus, they sometimes poll other vessels that heard the call to try to triangulate an approximate position. If you can give them a time, signal strength, and your own position, the information can be invaluable in tracking down the vessel that needs help.

---

[49] You are logging your position regularly, right?

Advanced Radio Techniques

Once you are comfortable with the basic back and forth of a radio call, it's time to commit yourself to more advanced topics. These things aren't anything fancy, but they are tips and tricks that can take you from a basic radio user and turn you into a real radio star in no time at all.

To Radio or Not To Radio

Radio use is as much about understanding *when* to make a call as how. Novice users may agonize over whether or not they should put out a Securité call. A sign of polish is not worrying about it so much; like deciding to shorten sail in rising wind conditions, if it crosses your mind, you should just do it. If you're following the guidance we've given you here, it's going to be short and to the point, and the worst that can happen is no one will care!

Appropriate use can vary a lot based on circumstances. Being tuned in to what is going on in your area can offer you a lot of flexibility in how you use your radio.

For example, conducting a long conversation on one of the five designated working channels about how the fishing is going some fine spring morning might be perfectly acceptable in some remote anchorage out of range of all but a handful of other boats. If it's the opening day of salmon season on Puget Sound, with hundreds of cruisers and fishing boats around, it's a lot less defensible. It's as if you're in a prison with a bank of only five phones, and 200 other prisoners are standing behind you waiting to make their weekly call home. Every minute you are on the line, you're keeping someone else from using it.

In the same vein, advanced users will know when they can ninja into a channel even when it's ostensibly being used already. Way back in Hailing and Answering, we told you that when someone is making a call on a hailing channel, the responsible thing for other parties to do is to wait until the called station has answered or until the caller has cleared the air.

Well, in busy areas, if you did that, you'd just never get your own call out. A lot of other users aren't going to be following protocol. They'll jam the air with calls every five seconds instead of leaving a gap for an answer. They won't clear off when no answer was received after three tries.

In those situations, you sort of just have to pick your moment. Slide in between those deaf old fishermen and use some of the suggestions from our Advanced Protocol section to make correct, but quick, calls of your own.

Radio Checks

We noted the existence and potential use of automated radio check systems earlier as a way to learn how you sound and practice transmitting on the radio. But radio checks, whether automated or manual, actually have their own legitimate function in the realm of radio use, which is to, well, check your radio. Go figure.

This is done by making a test transmission to another station, hopefully at a known range, and getting an assessment of your signal strength and quality from the receiver. The range matters because you would expect to have a lousy readability at 30 or 40 miles; that doesn't necessarily tell you anything about your radio setup. If you are hard to read at 10 miles, well, something is probably wrong.

With automated systems, this is done just by retransmitting your own transmission back to you—you can decide how it sounds when you hear it played back. Those systems have some deficiencies, though. You don't really know how loud or clear the signal came through initially. When it is played back to you, any problems you hear could have originated on the other end.

A human listener can assess your transmission more effectively. The only problem is finding a listener. Radio checks have become something of a nuisance on hailing channels, cluttering up the airwaves with anxious new users trying to figure out whether their set is working. In the United States, the Coast Guard frowns heavily on radio checks made on customary hailing and distress frequencies. If they respond, it will mostly be to scold you and get you off the air.

But the Coast Guard is the natural choice to call for radio checks because you know they are listening at all hours, and you can figure out where they are transmitting from pretty easily, too (giving you a known range).

In many sectors, watchstanders will take your radio checks on the primary USCG working channel, 22A, when it's not occupied with other traffic.[50]

Coast Guard Sector San Francisco, Coast Guard Sector San Francisco, this is *Serenity, Serenity,* calling for a radio check on Two Two Alpha, over.

Vessel *Serenity*, this is Coast Guard Sector San Francisco, we have you loud and clear on Two Two Alpha, out.

Assessing The Quality Of A Transmission

"Loud and clear," incidentally, is one way of evaluating a transmission (the way you hope it will be heard, in fact!), but

---

[50] The official policy on this, as of 2019, is that the US Coast Guard will take radio checks via DSC and HF radios... no mention is made of old-fashioned VHF. Though they are trying to discourage this sort of general airwave clutter, in practice many watchstanders will reply.

The Canadian Coast Guard is altogether more understanding and will calmly answer most radio check calls on either 16 or their regional working frequency. Because you're a responsible radio user who reads the footnotes, you know to try them on the working frequency first.

there are other possible replies. "Weak and broken" is one, or the station might try to give you a more complete breakdown of why you sound unreadable.

But old-school watchstanders will often use a different, more subtle scale—one that you can use, too, if you ever happen to be on the receiving end of a radio check call.

Instead of "loud and clear," you'll sometimes hear "I have you five by five."

This is a two-part numeric scale from one to five where the first number is your readability, and the second is signal strength. So if you get, "*Serenity*, I have you two by four," you know that you are sending a strong signal (four out of five ain't bad) and are loud enough, but that interference, distortion, or some other issue is making your actual words difficult to understand.

Combined with knowing the location of the receiver, this can give you great troubleshooting information. A strong signal at a great distance means your transmitter is working well, sending a powerful transmission out that is easy to pick up. If there are issues of clarity, that can point toward your own mumbling, dust in your microphone, or distortion introduced by feedback somewhere on your boat.

Cool Radio Slang

So jargon is a mixed bag, but almost all of us employ it in our daily lives to a greater or lesser extent. Just about every profession, hobby, or avocation has its own unique lexicon of technical terminology or idiom that outsiders are unfamiliar with, but that mark users as members of the club.

Radio is no different, and, as with any sort of jargon, you can sound like a real idiot if you use it incorrectly. It's definitely a step for advanced users only… don't step into these terms until you are feeling very comfortable on the radio.

Yet, once you do, being able to use them, or other, regional linguistic contrivances, will both aid comprehension and give you new verbal tools to sound smoother and get your point across faster in any radio conversation.

Up and Down for Channels

It's common in some areas to use "up" and "down" as sort of informal pro words. If you and *Velcro* were chatting away on channel 68 and someone suddenly burst into your conversation (or vice versa), you might quickly tell *Velcro* to move up to channel 69.

> *Velcro*, let's go up one.

Spelling it Out

From time to time, you will end up having to spell something over the air. If you chose poorly when you named your boat, this will happen a lot! In these moments, you will find yourself wishing you had studied the phonetic alphabet more closely.

Because you probably won't do that, it's a good idea to keep a printout handy near your radio. You'll find it easy to pick up the trick of looking up the right word as you spell because you should be reading them off slowly anyway. For words you find yourself spelling out phonetically very commonly (like *Knotty Bouyz*), just go ahead and print out the phonetic versions of those words and put them up individually.

Start the spelled word with the pro word "I spell."

> *Serenity*, Oak Bay Marina, can you spell your vessel name for me, please?
>
> Roger, Oak Bay, *Serenity* is, I spell, Sierra Echo Romeo Echo November India Tango Yankee, over.

If you just flat out don't have the "official" phonetic alphabet handy, most folks will understand if you just fall back on the "D is for Dog, Z is for Zebra" technique of using any common word that starts with that letter that you can think of.

Numbers

Numbers are a slightly different story. They don't have a separate word for each because they are already separate words, but some of those can be hard to understand over the air. The accepted way to be clear with reading off numbers is to deliberately mispronounce some of them:

0 ZE-RO
1 WUN
2 TOO
3 TREE
4 FOW-ER
5 FIFE
6 SIX
7 SEV-EN
8 AIT
9 NIN-ER

A dash represents a syllable, so "fow-er," for example, has two distinct sounds in it, unlike "four." These are sometimes called phonetic numbers.

Getting over "over"

You might have noticed in a few of our recent examples there has been no "over" pro word at the appropriate place in the transmission. That's because it's perfectly fine to drop it as needless overhead where conditions don't require it. If you say "go ahead" the "over" is pretty much implicit, isn't it? Similarly, when you are making any relatively plain, short statement resembling a basic English sentence in normal conditions, the person on the other end is going to recognize when it's their turn to talk after you drop the carrier. In probably *most* VHF conversations, "over" just never gets used... and no one even notices.

PHONETICS

The pesky fact that English has a number of letters that sound similar to one another has been a problem since before radio was even invented. The military, which had a vested interest in getting things like artillery barrages right on the first try, was first to take a stab at a phonetic spelling alphabet for use over phone lines. The British War Office Signaling Instructions of 1898 called for signalers to replace a handful of commonly misunderstood letters with keywords that would be less likely to be misunderstood over poor connections: Ack, Beer, eMma, Toc.

This practice was refined during the Great War, but World War II, which saw the widespread use of radio communications in all theaters and between allies of various nationalities and accents, really drove home the need for standardization. The Joint Army/Navy Phonetic Alphabet was adopted in 1941 and used by the Allies exclusively from 1943 through the end of the war.

During the same period, air traffic had surged and also had the need to ensure accurate communication between pilots and ground stations internationally. Taking their cue from the Joint Alphabet, the International Civil Aviation Organization conducted exhaustive listening tests after the war to determine the most easily understood spelling words and issued their International Radiotelephony Spelling Alphabet in 1956. It was promptly adopted by NATO (the North Atlantic Treaty Organization established by the Western allies after the war) and subsequently all member militaries and thus quickly became the default spelling alphabet for Latin letters worldwide.

It is technically a spelling alphabet, despite commonly being called a phonetic alphabet.[51] Nor is it the only spelling alphabet. APCO, the Association of Public Safety Communications Officials, developed their own version in the 1940s together with the 10-Codes once commonly used by police, which is why the TV show was called "Adam-12" and not "Alpha-12." But even boat cops use the NATO version today.

The NATO/ICAO standard that you will use for marine radio is:

A - Alpha	N - November
B - Bravo	O - Oscar
C - Charlie	P - Papa
D - Delta	Q - Quebec

---

[51] A real phonetic alphabet shows the pronunciation of words themselves—the phonemes—rather than letters used to spell them.

E - Echo	R - Romeo
F - Foxtrot	S - Sierra
G - Golf	T - Tango
H - Hotel	U - Uniform
I - India	V - Victor
J - Juliet	W - Whiskey
K - Kilo	X - X-ray
L - Lima	Y - Yankee
M - Mike	Z - Zulu

Advanced Radio Protocols

They say you have to know the rules in order to break them. Of course, that's obviously not the case—you can listen to people breaking the rules of proper radio protocol all the time simply because they don't know any better.

But it is true that you can learn to break the rules in order to serve the underlying interest more directly, and you will hear people doing that all the time, too. In fact, breaking the rules[52] in the right way is exactly what will mark you as a radio pro and not just some lubber out for a once-a-year day sail.

Balancing Clarity With Brevity

Since you understand that radio procedure is about clarity and brevity, you know that there is some tension between the two. Using more words, a longer transmission, is more likely to result in a clear message, but at the expense of brevity, and vice versa. Radio protocol, as you've learned, seeks to balance these against one another.

But protocol is designed around some theoretical case that isn't always applicable in the real world. Conditions can be better or worse, the air can be busier or less busy, at any given time. You're not some mindless robot. You can evaluate the two requirements against one another and make a decision about which is more important in a certain moment.

Perhaps more importantly, once you learn these tricks, you will also understand how to respond when someone else uses them—as professional mariners and experienced yachtsmen do all the time. You'll be part of that club, a steward of the airwaves, the cool kid on the block.

---

[52] "Well, more what you'd call guidelines than actual rules." — Captain Barbossa

Removing Repetition

One of the most common and practical ways of clearing the air faster is to eliminate repetition in conditions where it isn't warranted. Consider the following conversation, all letter-perfect:

Velcro, Velcro, Velcro, this is *Serenity, Serenity, Serenity,* over.
Serenity, this is *Velcro,* over.
Velcro, Serenity. Let's shift to channel 68, over.
Serenity, Velcro. Switching to channel 68, out.

Now, the way the same conversation could happen in most cases, where reception is good and the vessels moderately familiar with one another:

Velcro, Serenity, over.
Serenity, Velcro.
Velcro, switch and answer 68.

The resulting conversation is just as clear, but takes only a quarter of the time — clarity and brevity have both been served.

Let's look at why this works by diagramming these three simple lines out:

Velcro, Serenity, over.	The initial call only ever requires identifying the hailed and hailing stations. Once that's accomplished, in good conditions, repetition is unnecessary.

Serenity, Velcro.	The reply indicates the initial hail has been heard; "over" is implied because the hailing station will be the one introducing the topic of conversation next.
Velcro, switch and answer 68.	Changing channels implies "out."

But there are further efficiencies to be had. *Velcro*, knowing that the conversation will have to be shifted to a working channel anyway, simply proposes the channel themselves:

Velcro, Serenity.
Serenity, 68.
Roger.

It's convention to repeat the station name three times, but unnecessary most of the time. In fact, the International Code of Signals notes only that you should repeat the name *not more than three times*.[53] If one of the vessels has a particularly hard-to-understand name or reception quality is poor, then by all means go for three. Otherwise, you can usually keep it to one or two — if you've already been in contact or are hailing someone who you know is expecting the call, one is almost always plenty.

There are dozens of ways to create shorter radio calls, most of them simply by dropping words or parts of the conversation that you can assume both parties already know. Consider this part of an exchange from earlier in the book:

---

[53] The Code of Signals is a wonderful read that is not only the source of insights such as this but also such gems as which combination of nautical signal flags you should fly if you have had a serious nuclear accident on board... Alpha Juliet, in case you ever need to know.

Vessel calling the 40-foot white boat in position 46 degrees 15.2 minutes North by 126 degrees 1 minute West, this is the 46-foot Bayliner *Serenity*, over.

Unless you are using the most powerful transmitter in the world, chances are everybody knows that the coordinates are North and West. The exact length is irrelevant to the rest of the conversation. And the numbers involved are a repetition of coordinates already provided, so it can be assumed that when you say them, you are giving a lat/long again.

Bearing all that in mind, your reply could be shortened to:

Vessel calling the white boat at 46 15 by 126 1, this is *Serenity*, over.

Or, if you're pretty darn sure you're the only boat that could be the recipient, simply:

Vessel calling, this is *Serenity*, over.

You're giving everyone enough information to proceed with the conversation, but not unnecessarily clogging up the air.

You may also have noticed that we told you originally that all radio calls other than Maydays must be directed at some other station. Then we went and gave an example of a Securité call without naming one! But that's because a Securité without a named target implicitly is directed to all stations. It's perfectly accurate to incorporate that into such a call (and we used other examples that did so), but you can also save a little air time by omitting it and no one is going to be confused about it.

Rarely Used But Useful Protocols

There are also the rare, but useful, little nuggets of radio protocol you can break out from time to time both to save yourself some time and to sound really cool doing it.

Hassle-free Hailing

On any busy summer weekend, it can be a real chore to find an opening on regular hailing channels. This is exactly the reason the FCC added channel 9 as an alternate hailing channel for recreational craft.

But if you have a friend or group of other boats that you know you will be contacting regularly, you can both avoid and alleviate the problem by agreeing to listen in on an alternate channel as well. Of course, this has to be an approved channel for the traffic you will be sending. But there is no law against hailing someone directly on a working frequency. And that channel is more likely to be open in the first place since fewer people will be on it by default.

This doesn't relieve you of your responsibility to monitor channel 16, but with the ability of modern radios to listen in scan mode, that's no real obstacle to doing both.

Taking Some Breaks

Sometimes, you have a real mouthful to get out in a transmission, but you need to catch your breath. Or, you lose the thread along the way and need a second to collect your thoughts, but haven't finished speaking your piece just yet.

The "break" pro word is made for these situations. It lets listeners know that you are going to release your mike key but plan to continue transmitting shortly, so they should not interrupt.

Don't abuse this; you shouldn't take more than a few seconds before resuming your transmission. You don't need to do anything special, just resume transmitting as if you'd never released the mike button—you don't even have to identify yourself again.

Break can also be used simply to segment your conversations

without actually stopping the transmission. If, for example, you have been in conversation with one station and find that you immediately need to contact another, you can say "break" before hailing them. You'll hear the Coast Guard use break in this sense frequently during long transmissions when they want to separate different topics.

You can also use break when you want to continue controlling the air but want to hail a station other than the one you are currently addressing. You are "breaking" off your conversation with the first station, but plan to maintain control of the air and immediately hail a second station.

There's another use of "break" that is considerably more rare and should only be used in emergencies (although you will hear the Coast Guard using it to horn in on illegal transmissions from time to time). That is to interject into someone else's active transmission with your own.

Obviously, this is strongly discouraged and should probably only be done when you need to get a distress or urgency message out.

Clearing the Channel

You already know that when you are done with a conversation, you clear the air by using the "out" pro word.

But this leaves some ambiguity about where you are going "out" to. If you did the right thing and moved to a working channel after making your initial connection, are you continuing to monitor it? Or are you switching it off and going back to a designated hailing frequency? Since most radios can monitor multiple channels today, it's an open question, but you can answer it easily when you clear out.

Serenity `clearing to 16.`

Or:

Serenity back to 16, out.

Staying in Touch With Contact Schedules

From time to time, it may be important to ensure that you are able to contact someone on a regular basis, but either you or they can't continuously monitor the air. Rather than fruitlessly hailing the aether at random intervals, the right way to handle this is to set up a contact schedule.

This is as simple as coming to an agreement on a time and channel you will mutually monitor for making contact. For example, you might arrange to meet on 4149kHz at five past the hour every odd hour, or each day at noon GMT... whatever makes sense for your communication needs.

This doesn't prevent you from connecting more frequently, but it provides a venue where you will more likely than not be able to reliably contact one another.

Radio nets are one type of contact schedule. RCCs (Rescue Coordination Centers) also routinely set up contact schedules with vessels in distress for a slightly different reason; they want to ensure they are receiving regular updates on the status and position. If for some reason that vessel misses a contact time, rescuers will at least have the last known position and a somewhat recent picture of the situation, making rescue attempts more likely to end up in the right area.

You don't have to be so rigorous or worry much if you miss a meeting, but contact schedules can be a useful tool for even routine communication.

Ahoy, Skipper

This isn't actually all that rare, but it might require some explanation. You may, depending on where you do your boating, more or less frequently hear parties on the radio referring to one another, or even to you, as "skip," "skipper," or "captain."

You being a recreational boater, and probably not one with a master's ticket, may not think of yourself as being a captain, but there's a difference between the terms: a ship's master has a professional qualification with an official regulatory meaning, while "captain" (or the "skipper" analog) is an informal term that simply refers to the person currently in control of a vessel. Assuming yours *is* in control,[54] then it has a captain, whether it be a kayak or a mega-yacht. And referring to that person as captain or skipper or skip or whatever the local variant may be is simply a courtesy and convention in many areas. You can adopt it when conversing with other vessels, and shouldn't be shocked when they use it with you.

Saying "Copy" With Two Clicks

When receiving a non-critical transmission, it's possible to acknowledge receipt by quickly clicking the mike button twice. You are not saying anything, just breaking the carrier—it comes across as two short bursts of static on receiving sets. Almost always, this happens during the final transmission of a conversation, where your reply may not strictly be necessary, and you expect no further traffic.

Outside of the military, this is so uncommon we wouldn't recommend using it with random stations, but it's perfectly fine for use between friends, and if someone else happens to use it while conversing with you, now you'll know what it means.

---

[54] And note that "in control" does not necessarily mean "at the helm." The person making the decisions under which the vessel is operating is the skipper, regardless of other divisions of duties on board.

Common Radio Problems

There are some very common problems that you will hear repeatedly as you listen to radio traffic. You may even find that you are experiencing a few of them yourself as you are getting started with marine radio. Fortunately, they all have simple solutions.

Volume levels too low or too loud

If people can barely hear you, chances are you are either whispering into the microphone or holding it too far from your mouth. A few inches is good. You should also be speaking at normal conversational volumes—the radio is calibrated to send at those levels, it won't automatically amplify your voice.

On the other end of the scale, sometimes you may be sending out such a loud signal that it distorts reception on the other end. So don't yell in the mike and don't hold it too close.

The Rule of Thumb: When you're holding the microphone in your hand, stick your thumb out straight from the mouthpiece. If your thumb hits your chin, you're too close!

An easy way to keep from eating the mic... if the thumb hits, you're too close.

Other noises drowning out the radio

Sometimes, you'll just have trouble hearing the radio, or, even if your levels are okay, people you are talking to won't be able to understand you. This is often due to background noise on either end. If it's on the other end, you can't do much about it, but if the source is on your end, there are a few things to think about.

Radio microphones are not precision instruments. They will pick up whatever noise wanders into them. Keep this in mind if you are speaking from a position next to a running engine or in a windy cockpit. You might want to shield the mike by turning to face the source of the noise (which will put it *behind* the microphone). If you have noisy guests, shush them for the duration of your conversation.

Failing to listen long enough before or between hailing calls

This is so common it almost doesn't bear mentioning… you'll constantly hear inexperienced users calling another vessel, then repeating the call again two seconds later. Or, they'll just jump into the middle of someone else's call without having listened to see if the channel was in use first.

It goes without saying that you should avoid this behavior yourself.

On the other hand, if everyone is managing the channel responsibly, it's entirely possible to overlap hailing calls without causing conflict. It's not recommended, but if another vessel is not having any luck getting ahold of their recipient, you can sometimes dart in your own call quickly without disrupting anything.

More commonly, other vessels won't clear off the channel to signal to you that it's okay to use it. So you just have to use your judgment on this subject anyway.

Overtalking

This is more of a problem than you might imagine. Some people have trouble getting the first word out once they pick up the mike; others just can't seem to stop talking even when they've run out of things to say. They just don't realize when they have reached the end of their sentence or aren't sure quite how to wrap it up.

The best cure for this is to compose what you will say ahead of time, but that's not always possible. Some of us just don't think on our feet fast enough to put together a reply in a reasonable amount of time.

But give that a try first. You don't *have to* reply immediately; ten or twenty seconds isn't really that long in a radio conversation. Cut yourself some slack and think about the conversation for a second.

If you get in trouble mid-transmission, there's a handy trick to get out of it: break. As discussed in Advanced Protocol, you can use the "break" pro word at any time to keep control of the air but stop transmitting. If you find yourself stumbling over a particularly bad series of "uhs" and "ummms," knock it off as soon as you notice:

> We saw a few of those kind of black and white porpoises... the kind that, uh... you know, they look like little killer whales? Um, the ones that... uh... break.

Go look up the name and start talking when you figure out what you want to say.[55]

Transmitting on the wrong channel

A lack of familiarity with the area you are operating in or the target of your transmission can easily turn you into one of the most pathetic of radio users: the frustrated one who never gets an answer.

There are a couple of common causes for this faux pas on VHF:

- **Not checking customary channels for shore stations** — Shore stations (such as marinas) are not required to monitor 16, and much of the traffic there isn't relevant to them, so

---

[55] They are called Dall's porpoises, by the way.

they frequently pick a different channel to monitor. In some cases, this is a loosely organized regional custom, while in others it's just an arbitrary selection. In either case, you may have to consult boaters' guides or other resources to figure out how to reach them. Your Local Notice to Mariners[56] can be invaluable in this respect—notices about channels being used during special events and operations (like construction or dredging) are often published there. A Special Notice to Mariners is also published by some Coast Guard Districts, which should include a chapter on Communications that lists common channels used in that district for VTS and other purposes.

- **Not understanding VTS operations** — When participating in a VTS scheme, vessels are generally also not required to monitor 16, even if they are otherwise legally obligated to do so. You can't tell just by looking if a vessel is using VTS or not, but you can often make logical deductions: in heavily trafficked areas, deep draft vessels hewing to a designated lane are almost certainly in VTS. If so, you'll have better luck reaching them on the VTS channel for that area or on bridge-to-bridge (Channel 13).

With SSB, this is less a screw-up and more part-and-parcel of the technology—wavebands are numerous and transmission qualities inexact. You rarely transmit on a channel unless you are fairly sure someone you want to reach will be there, but that's no guaranty of reaching them, pending range and atmospheric conditions.

Forgetting to identify yourself

This is a surprisingly common problem, and, unlike most of the others listed here, seems to afflict experienced radio users more than neophytes. Maybe you just get too comfortable on the radio after a while and forget you're not chatting face-to-face. Or

---

[56] Each U.S. Coast Guard District publishes their own regional Notice to Mariners, all of which can be located from the central website www.navcen.uscg.gov.

maybe it's just natural... you know who you are, after all; why wouldn't everyone else?

But it's a mistake that causes a lot of miscommunication since even if you have managed to identifiably hail another station, you are giving them trouble in replying. They have to fall back on the old "Vessel calling so-and-so..." routine, which may simply lead to more issues since suddenly neither of you are sure who you are talking to.

The only remedy is to identify yourself as soon as you realize you haven't yet. Although you should do so at the start of the call, a belated, "Oh, by the way, this is *Serendipity*" is better than no identification at all.

General Screw-ups

It's inevitable—you're gonna screw things up sooner or later while you've got the mike keyed. It happens to everyone. Your brain glitches or you didn't practice enough or something creates a distraction, and you botch a transmission... usually something really embarrassing like:

```
Copy that, Coast Guard, we're approaching
the accident site now to render assistance
and... GODDAMMIT, Edith! My OTHER captain's
hat, the one with the gold braid... oh shit...
break.
```

Or you have one of those brain freezes where you forget what you were saying mid-sentence and just sit there, your thumb glued to the button, dead air propagating out over the waves with the seconds ticking by as everyone in the area listens in breathlessly, waiting for that profound message that you just... can't... quite... seem... to say.

Just remember, none of them can see the expression on your face at that moment.

The most important thing is to let go of that key. The longer you keep stumbling, blustering, or not saying a word, the worse you're going to feel. Put the world on mute for a second and take a moment to get composed. You're going to start over again, just like you practiced:
- Take a deep breath
- Think about what you need to communicate
- Rehearse it in your head
- Key the mike and say it like you're talking to a store clerk

You can't fix what has already been transmitted, but you can continue so smoothly that people will forget there was ever a problem in the first place.

Corrections

There are also easy ways to deal with screw-ups while your transmission is in progress. Everyone misspeaks from time to time, just as in normal conversations. And just like in regular conversations, you're allowed to correct yourself in mid-stream... in fact, there's a pro word just for that purpose, which is, in fact, "correction."

> Coast Guard, *Serenity*, our current position is approximately 10 miles south of Monomoy Point... correction, 10 miles south of Point Gammon...

You may also hear people use another term, "check that" although it's less common and may be somewhat confusing to people without a military radio background. But it can be used in the same sense as correction.

> *Velcro, Serenity*, understand you will be passing on our starbo... check that, on our port side, over?

ON RADIO RAGE

Hopefully, it's already been made completely clear to you that it's a real no-no to make any broadcast without putting your name to it. But you'll hear people doing just that all the time in any busy harbor or sea lane… usually to squawk at someone nearby doing something of which they don't approve.

The temptation is powerful, such as when a teal Trophy sport fishing boat blasts across your bow at full speed as you are dropping sail single-handed at the entrance to Prevost Harbor, slamming the rig around, slopping folds of loose sailcloth everywhere, and hopelessly tangling all the control lines as you hang onto the swaying boom for dear life.[57] Being unequipped with torpedos, the radio is really the only other way to reach out and touch such scourges of the seas.

Except the reality is that such jerks probably don't closely monitor their radios anyway, and, even if they did, would almost certainly assume you were talking to someone else. In the meantime, you've laced profanity or bad vibes across a spectrum of other innocent listeners, stomping on perfectly respectable conversations or preventing others from starting. Who is the jerk now?

The anonymity that comes with radio traffic you don't bless with your call sign provides a similar cover to what most people have on the internet every day. And we've all seen how civil and courteous that venue has become!

So do yourself and everyone around you a favor, even when you are gripped in the depths of perfectly justifiable rage… if it's not something you're willing to say with your identity attached, just don't say it at all.

---

[57] Why, of course this is a purely theoretical example! Why do you ask?

CHAPTER FOUR
Operation and Troubleshooting

Understanding Marine Radio Technology

We promised not to get overly technical with you in this book, and hopefully you have found that to be the case so far. But now that you're nearly at the end, there's a little caveat... to be a really comfortable and competent user of VHF, you honestly do need to know a little bit about how that black box works.

While most of you are going to be using radios that someone else installed, and will probably have a technician install any new radio that you might get, you can't get away from the fact that you may well experience problems with the radio when you are far from professional assistance. In those cases, the only available troubleshooter will be you, and you better have some idea where to start, or you're going to get nowhere when you need to call for help.

It's also the case that it's hard to assess the work that someone else does for you if you don't even have the first clue about how the system works.

So in this section, we're going to talk a little bit—really, the bare minimum!—about how the pieces of a VHF system go together and what the considerations are when either installing or troubleshooting a radio system. We're going to talk a bit about the features to look for on modern VHF sets, and about the other radios you might have on board and how they can either integrate or interfere with your VHF. And we'll discuss the radio spectrum underpinning marine VHF and why it's such a popular and effective choice for marine communication.

Very High Frequency: Your Basic Radio

For most boaters, "the radio" is simply going to be a typical, off-the-shelf VHF set, so that's where we'll start.

VHF stands for "Very High Frequency." It's a frequency band (30 MHz to 300 MHz) that has characteristics that are well-suited to short-range communication.
- The waves are usually restricted to the local radio horizon, usually less than 50 miles, but are not strictly line-of-sight... they can penetrate some foliage and structures.
- The frequency range is not as susceptible to atmospheric noise and electrical interference as lower frequency ranges.
- Transmissions do not require a great deal of power.
- Antenna length is not unwieldy.

This combination results in a relatively robust communication platform that is not overpowering. While the range restriction might seem a liability at first, in practice it allows VHF use to be much more widespread and less busy than if it reached further — if boaters in Boston had to share the airwaves with those in New York, for example, there would have to be a lot more discipline and restrictions to keep the air open. It would be less useful for everyone.

All these factors make VHF a pretty popular frequency range for a multitude of different uses. In addition to marine communication, the VHF band is also used for:
- Broadcast television
- FM radio
- Aircraft coordination and operation
- Military communications
- Cordless phones and ham radio
- Public safety radio

All those uses are kept from conflicting with one another by a plan of channels and frequencies that keep them separate. Because the radios for each segment are built to comply with the rules, you don't need to worry about anything outside of the marine band.

Aircraft are permitted to use some marine VHF channels, but only for the purposes of communicating with boats. Because of their altitude, their sets have great range and would interfere with boaters over a wide area if used regularly, so they are generally restricted to making contact for safety or law enforcement purposes on a small subset of channels.[58]

Frequencies and Channels

By international convention, the frequency range between 156 and 174 Megahertz (MHz) is reserved for maritime use.

In certain very rare circumstances, you might see a frequency referred to directly, like 156.800 MHz—the international hailing and distress communication frequency.

But mostly, you will only see or care about the channels that these frequencies have been divided into... 156.800 MHz , for instance, being Channel 16.

Because VHF uses frequency modulation, the actual transmissions constantly go back and forth on either side of that theoretical frequency. So a gap of .25 MHz is left on either side of 156.800 MHz to avoid interference.

There are about 60 of these channels,[59] interleaved and spread within the assigned range to avoid interfering with one another.[60] Periodically, advances in technology or needs result in a renumbering or repurposing of these channels. For example, as this book was being written, the Coast Guard and FCC (Federal Communication Commission) are in the process of revising the

---

[58] Oh, you *really* want to know what they are? Fine:
06, 08, 09, 16, 18, 22A, 67, 68, 72, 88

[59] So why does your dial go up to 88? Because there's a channel gap between 28 and 60 of unassigned numbers.

[60] This scheme is drawn up and administered by the International Telecommunication Union (ITU), which is the United Nation's agency that coordinates international spectrum use. The most current allocation of frequencies to channels, and approved uses, is found in Circular Letter CM/19.

U.S. VHF channel plan to give 18 existing channels new channel numbers.

Because channel numbers are arbitrary, they don't necessarily have anything to do with the underlying sequence of frequencies. Channels are slightly different between the U.S., Canada, and international standards. The frequency for channel 2, for instance, isn't used in the U.S. And the U.S. uses part of the international channel 83 for its own 83A, while Canada takes another part and also adds an 83B... which the U.S. does not.

The reason these channels can be split up that way is that most of them were originally designed to be *duplex* instead of simplex. In other words, to allow you to talk and listen simultaneously, like a cell phone. And in order to accomplish that, you need two frequencies, one for each station.

While it sounds like a great idea, duplex communication never really caught on in a big way in marine communications, so reusing the secondary frequency has allowed communication regulators to squeeze more bandwidth out of the existing marine frequency allocation.

The ability of new radios to transmit and receive within even narrower frequency ranges is allowing more efficient use of the available bandwidth. Instead of a .25 MHz gap, new channels only have .125 MHz between them. These new channels are numbered in the 200 range, interleaved into existing frequency allocations, but are not available (as of 2017) in the U.S.

Features and Settings

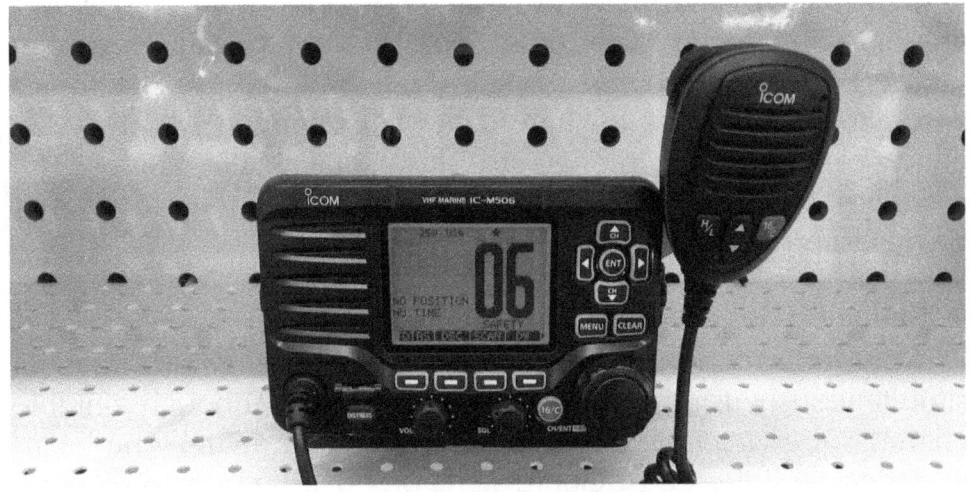

Modern VHF radios are starting to come out of the box with so many bells and whistles that they are starting to look like your home video player. If they had clocks, they'd be flashing "12:00" on most boats—or "No Position, No Time" as you see here.[61]

This is just an overview of the general types of features that are commonly available today; it's not likely to be exhaustive and it won't tell you how to adjust the settings on your specific radio—you should refer to the manual, since every manufacturer has their own unique and infuriating way of doing things.

Display Screens

When the features on a radio start to outstrip the panel space available for buttons, manufacturers have begun to incorporate LCD screens to help you see all the settings and operate the controls. The screens also double as displays for AIS and DSC transmission information (see below).

---

[61] Actually, many of them do have clocks and most of those are set automatically by integrated GPS receivers. But you get the point. At least if you are old enough to remember what a VCR is.

Interfaces

Many other capabilities are available on modern radios when they are interfaced with other boat systems. Many high-end radios accept or provide NMEA (National Marine Electronics Association) interfaces to share data on a common bus. This can allow capable chart plotters to show DSC call locations on screen, or for an external GPS to provide fixes to the radio for its own DSC broadcasts.

Scanning Modes and Alerts

Most radios have the ability to monitor more than one channel simultaneously using dual or tri-watch features. Although multiple channels are watched, only one broadcast can actually be heard at a time, so if the Coast Guard starts broadcasting on 16, you are going to miss your friend hailing you on Channel 9 at the same time. These modes usually allow a priority designation, so you can pick a channel to "win" in the event that transmissions come in on more than one at a time.

Weather alert tones broadcast on the NOAA WX channels will also trigger some radios to automatically switch over to and play critical weather updates.

Remote Microphone stations

High-end radios sometimes have the capability to wire in other microphone stations in addition to the main unit. These remote mikes have some limited control features built in so you can change volume and channel remotely as well. This is a handy setup both for sailboats, which often have the main VHF unit installed below but whose crews are usually up in the cockpit and for powerboats with flybridge stations in addition to the main helm.

Noise-canceling

Noise-canceling radios used feedback methods similar to those in noise-canceling audio headphones to remove background noise from wind, waves, and engines from radio calls. They work both on calls you make, so it sounds clearer on the other end, and those you receive.

Call recording

Another fancy feature on high-end radios is automatic call recording. Every mariner has had the experience of getting a transmission that is just too fuzzy to understand, or flat out missing what is said because of a distraction or ill-timed seagull screech. This feature allows instant rewind and replay of the last few minutes of any transmission so you can listen again to try to make it out.

Multiple Channel plan capability

Almost all radios have the ability to receive all the internationally-recognized VHF channels. Some allow you to switch back and forth between American, Canadian, and International channel plans as you round the world, making communication with the locals a little easier.

AIS Integration

The Automatic Identification System is a system that allows vessels underway to directly broadcast information about their course, speed, and intentions to help avoid collisions. This is not a voice communication system, but it uses VHF frequencies to transmit the information, and many radios now include the ability to receive and display data from nearby vessels.

We discuss the system in more detail in the Other Types of Radio overview section.

DIGITAL SELECTIVE CALLING

A relatively new feature makes hailing another station or transmitting an emergency message as easy as hitting a single button. Digital Selective Calling was introduced in 1983 and made mandatory on all new radios sold after 1999.[62] The feature uses a dedicated channel[63] to squirt high-speed, compressed digital signals over the air, which are intercepted and interpreted by other DSC-equipped radios. This feature can trigger alarms, selectively ring certain stations, and transfer information about the calling vessel and type of call being made.

DSC is a feature common to both VHF and SSB radios as part of the GMDSS (Global Maritime Distress and Safety System) system. They are not interchangeable—VHF radios cannot receive DSC calls from SSB sets, nor vice versa—but as a practical matter, they function the same way.

Each radio has a unique number, called an MMSI (Maritime Mobile Service Identity), which effectively serves as its phone number. And like phone numbers, there is a central registry of MMSI numbers, maintained by the ITU (International Telecommunications Union).

Registration of an MMSI is not automatic just because you buy a radio. You must register your DSC radio set with the proper authority for it to work correctly.

You have to register via an approved organization (such as BoatU.S. or Seatow) or directly with the FCC with your name and vessel information.[64] According to the Coast Guard, as of 2011, 90 percent of eligible boaters had not yet made that registration.

It's worth your while to do so, however, because the best feature of DSC—one-touch emergency broadcasts—relies on this. By registering your MMSI, you are effectively giving the Coast Guard much of the information that they will need in order to start

---

[62] Since you can still buy new handhelds either with or without DSC it seems they must be exempt; however, pouring through heaps of FCC documents in order to verify that fact, I wasn't able to find such a rule.

[63] VHF Channel 70

[64] Boat US offers a free MMSI registry service to members, but be careful—the numbers you obtain from them and other third party registrars may go only into a domestic database. If you subsequently plan to travel internationally, you will have to re-register directly with the FCC for a new MMSI, which will go into the international ITU database used by rescue agencies worldwide.

rescue operations:
- Your name, address, and telephone number (usually used to rule out false alarms)
- Your vessel name, description, capacity, and capabilities—all useful to rescuers
- Your EPIRB information, if you are so equipped

DSC radios often have another great feature, which is an ability to integrate with onboard GPS (Global Positioning System) units to automatically broadcast your location along with any distress call. This takes a huge factor in SAR (Search and Rescue) operations and makes it moot: establishing the location of the victim. In the adrenaline-filled moments of a real emergency, it is extremely difficult for most people to figure out where they are and successfully read that information out over the radio. Numerous rescue operations fail because an accurate position cannot be determined... helicopters, boats, and aircraft end up looking in the wrong spot.

In one swoop, that possibility is greatly minimized if you have a GPS-integrated DSC radio on board.

Some high-end VHF sets actually include a GPS receiver, so no additional connections are necessary.

Other Radios On Board

Although this book is mostly about how to use *voice* radio communications, there are a lot of other systems on most modern boats that make use of radios. In some cases, those will be interfaced directly to the VHF or SSB sets you have on board, so we'll touch on them as they can affect how your setup is wired or operated.

There are also some special purpose radio units you should be familiar with for safety purposes, such as EPIRBs (Emergency Position-Indicating Radio Beacon) and SARTs (Search And Rescue Transponder).

Finally, you should be aware of the different radios on your boat so you can track down and eliminate sources of interference that may be creating problems in your voice communications. We'll talk more about radio-frequency interference (RFI) in a bit; anything that transmits on board may be a suspect!

Ham and Single Sideband (SSB)

Long-distance cruisers make use of VHF radios as much as anyone, but they typically complement their equipment with more powerful, long-range transmitters that work in the Medium Frequency (MF) and High Frequency (HF) wave bands. These are either marine SSB radios or ham radios (the actual physical radios can typically transmit on channels accessible to both, but other restrictions apply), and require more extensive licensing and knowledge to use than a VHF. We deal with ham and SSB in our free to download SSB supplement to this guide, which you can find online at http://marineradio.forlubbers.com/.

Navtex

Navtex stands for NAVigational TELex, but no one remembers what a telex is these days so let's just keep it to Navtex, shall we?[65]

This is an information broadcast system operated by various national coast guards to provide weather and other navigational information. A Navtex receiver can be stand-alone or can tap into your SSB system since it is transmitted on shortwave frequencies.

NAVTEX receivers are preprogrammed to receive signals including all types of information broadcast by shore stations in 21 different Navareas around the globe. That information includes:

- Navigational and meteorological warnings (mandatory)
- Search and rescue information (mandatory)
- Ice reports, forecasts, and drill rig movement reports
- Pilot service messages, DECCA, LORAN, OMEGA, and satnav service reports

The mandatory information categories must be accepted by all receivers; other categories may be set to be ignored.

Old-style receivers were printers that recorded the transmissions on paper; newer receivers use LCD screens that allow you to scroll through the messages. Some computer programs also decipher NAVTEX now and can be installed on laptops that interface with receivers. NAVTEX units may require their own antenna, separate from other radios on the boat, but it's also possible to use a splitter switch to use a currently installed SSB antenna. This method can fry your receiver with the wrong setup, so consult a professional first!

Automatic Identification System (AIS)

AIS transceivers broadcast digital data over VHF frequencies[66] with information about a vessel's identity, position, course, and speed. If you have an AIS receiver, you can monitor these

---

[65] Because you youngsters were wondering, telex was a switched network of remote printers, like a telephone network, only for text instead of voice. What, you thought text messages were invented for your cell phone?

[66] Parts of channels 87 and 88, the unused shore station frequency of the original duplex channels. These are often labeled as AIS1 and AIS2 in modern channel plans.

broadcasts, and many radios or integrated chartplotters will display the information for you visually.

Most AIS users are commercial vessels. There are two classes of AIS transmitter:
- Class A — Complies with all IMO performance standards and carriage requirements; used by commercial vessels.
- Class B — Recreational transceivers, broadcasting at a lower power level and with fewer capabilities than the Class A units. Also less expensive than Class A. Class B is further divided into B-SO and B-CS, with B-CS being the cheapest, least powerful, and least capable transceivers, and B-SO representing a mid-range option.

But most recreational vessels do not actively participate in the AIS system. Instead, you are most likely to only install an AIS *receiver,* which allows you to receive both Class A and B signals but not to transmit your own information. Receivers are also much less expensive than transceivers. The downside, of course, is that commercial vessels will not see you on their AIS display.

Many modern DSC-equipped radios also have AIS reception and display capabilities. This makes installing AIS systems easy since they use your existing antenna and receiver without any additional hookups.

Otherwise, your installation will look something like this:

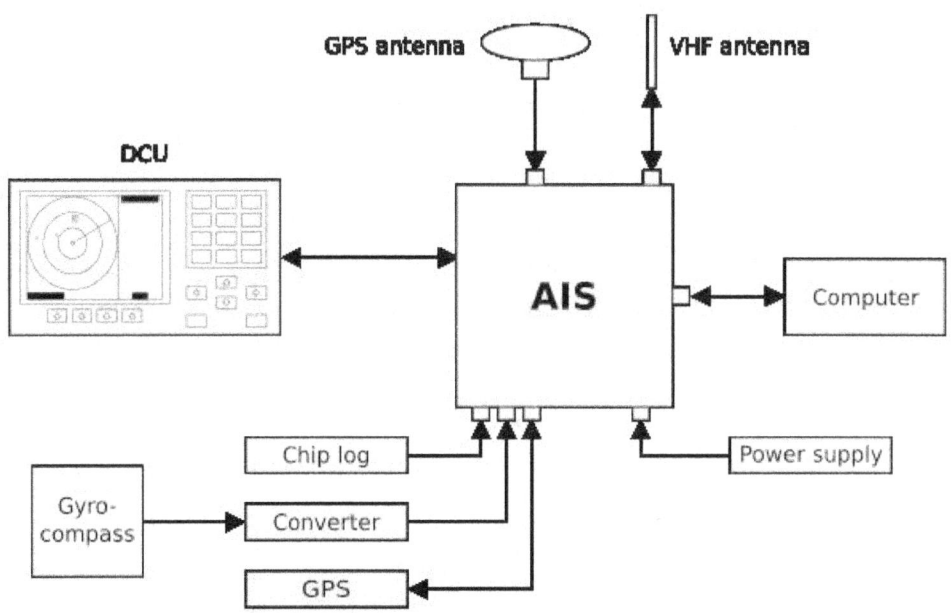

Image by Nicolas Lardot, Creative Common License, some rights reserved. [https://commons.wikimedia.org/w/index.php?curid=9064480]

Both of these systems tap into your existing VHF antenna, listening in for tiny, imperceptible fractions of a second that don't interfere with the regular use of your radio.

Like DSC, AIS relies on MMSI numbers to distinguish between ships. If you do install an AIS transmitter, you will use the MMSI from your DSC-equipped radio for AIS also. If you do not have a DSC radio, you will need to obtain an MMSI number separately for your AIS setup.

AIS MOB

A new use for the increasingly widespread network of AIS receivers is as a Man Overboard beacon. These are simply small, waterproof, ruggedized VHF transmitters (essentially very simplified handheld VHF units) that are pre-tuned to AIS frequencies and set to send a special code that will trigger AIS receivers to sound an alarm and indicate the MOBs position on the AIS display.

Although this is not as wide-reaching as a PLB, it has the advantage of putting MOB information directly into the hands of vessels in the best position to render immediate assistance—time is usually a critical factor to MOB survival. A PLB transmission will be received by a Rescue Coordination Center, but the RCC is usually hundreds or thousands of miles away—they have to re-transmit the information over their own radios and scramble rescuers from Coast Guard stations, but those processes take time.

EPIRB, SART, and PLB

These devices are all transmitters, but they only have one message: "Help! Here I am!" You can't control it other than to turn it on or off.

EPIRB/PLB

By design, EPIRBs are dead simple to use. With many of them, you don't need to do anything at all—the more sophisticated models have hydrostatic sensors built in that will trigger them automatically when they are submerged... presumably because the boat has sunk.

All of them, even those with automatic switches, can be triggered manually with the push of a single button.

Because they do not offer two-way communication, there's nothing more to do once you have set it off. The Rescue Coordination Center with responsibility for your area will likely attempt to contact you via VHF or SSB based on your registration information. If you have either type of radio accessible, listen on hailing frequencies and be ready to respond to provide details.

EPIRBs broadcast on a frequency monitor by a global satellite constellation. Normally, we wouldn't tell you what it is because who cares, but they changed the number a few years ago, and it's kind of important you get the right one. It's 406.025 MHz, and these are usually referred to as 406 EPIRBs.

But there's a trick; the old number was 121.5 MHz, and you actually want an EPIRB that broadcasts on *both* frequencies. This is because 121.5 MHz is a common aircraft guard channel, and every plane in the world can hear it. The 406 is good for getting to the satellite, which will tell a Rescue Control Center (RCC) that you have problems and give a rough location, but when they actually send some brave, burly rescue swimmers out for you in a plane or helicopter, that aircraft needs to be able to home in on you somehow.

A good EPIRB, in addition to having dual frequencies, will also have an integrated GPS to provide a good initial position to the RCC. It can reach satellites from any part of the globe and pinpoint your location within 4 minutes.

Personal Locator Beacons are basically man-portable EPIRBs. They have less power but work on the same frequencies and protocols and can be clipped onto a life jacket and activated in the event you go overboard.

SART

A Search And Rescue Transponder is a semi-active transceiver: when it is activated, it starts listening for signals from radar units. When it hears one, it transmits back on the same frequency in a code based on the signal strength. On the radar screen, it looks like this:

From left to right, the sequence of images shown as you first detect, approach, and finally identify the beacon location.
Image by the National Imagery and Mapping Agency [Public Domain]

This is another homing technology, giving rescuers a way to

find you when they get close. Because it responds to any X-band radar, even civilian vessels can see and use it. SARTs are often not much larger than AIS MOB or PLB devices but are usually intended to be included in life raft kits rather than as individual safety equipment.

SARTs may be a kind of radio that it is more important for you to recognize when someone else is using than to know how to use it yourself. After all, it's a one-button trigger for the user, but it relies on other people in the area (you, maybe!) recognizing the feedback it generates on a standard radar display, as shown above.

The line of dots, shown in the left-most frame, is what you will see at maximum range from the beacon—perhaps five miles. The dots show the direction of the beacon from your vessel.

Steering along that line will result, eventually, in receiving the series of arcs shown in the center frame. This indicates that you are within about a mile of the beacon.

As you keep moving toward the set of arcs, the arcs will shift into the series of concentric circles shown in the right-most frame. This indicates that you are right on top of the transponder, and it's time to stick your nose out of the cockpit and look around for the distress vessel itself.

Cellular and Satellite Phones

Any kind of phone that doesn't have a cord is also a radio, although we don't often think of them that way. They use duplex operations, so you can send and receive simultaneously, but otherwise include all the same limitations as other radios—power, hardware, and antenna.

Cellular

Because cell phones are optimized for land-based cellular networks, they don't work very well once you get outside of harbors. There are long lines of sight from coastal highlands where cell towers are likely to be located, but phones are designed to fit in your pocket, not to transmit over long distances.

The frequency ranges used were also selected with short-range use in mind. You're likely to lose signal when you get more than 20 to 40 miles away from land.

This also takes a toll on battery life. The weaker the signal, the harder the battery will be working.

On the plus side, they are the most familiar device you probably have on board, so using them comes very naturally.

Satellite

Satellite phones operate in a frequency range that allows them to reach up to satellites in orbit, which then relay the signal to ground stations that interface with the regular telephone network. They can be quite expensive and power-hungry.

On the other hand, they are also relatively easy to use, and most now offer some form of data transmission. This doesn't rival smartphone data use, but it is both easier and slightly faster to use than SSB packet radio systems.

Satphones are also a part of the GMDSS network. INMARSAT, the London-based International Maritime Satellite organization, was the first provider of civil marine satellite communications and provides mandatory services to SOLAS ships. The organization also uses its satellite constellation coverage to offer satellite phone and data service to private cruisers.

There are two other major satellite communications providers, Globalstar and Iridium.

All of these are expensive, and all have limitations based on the technologies they use and coverage techniques. INMARSAT, for example, provides service through four geostationary satellites positioned in line with the equator. This gives a very wide footprint, but not a tall one—coverage begins to fade at high latitudes, north or south of about 70 degrees. And equatorial orbital mechanics position the satellites at an altitude of 22,236 miles—a long way for a signal to travel, creating power and timing issues.

Globalstar and Iridium use birds that orbit between 500 and 900 miles up, making low-power transmitters more feasible—the inexpensive little SPOT tracker devices, for instance, uses the Globalstar network. But the low altitude makes for a more complicated orbit. Globalstar weaves together 24 satellites, and the pattern sometimes means that coverage is inconsistent far offshore, and entirely absent in some parts of the globe, such as the South Pacific.

Iridium has 66 satellites and uses polar orbits that make it the only provider that can offer complete global coverage at high latitudes.

Of course, coverage is only one consideration—cost, data speed, voice quality, equipment accessibility, and a host of other factors will weigh into your decision. You'll want to consult a professional when considering a satellite phone installation.

Because they are often only used intermittently, rental of portable sat phone equipment is also an option. While not as powerful as permanent ship installations, which have antennas fixed to your vessel, they are far less expensive and easier to evaluate.

Unlicensed Radio

This might seem confusing, because for most folks, a license isn't really necessary to use a VHF, either. But, historically, marine VHF was a licensed service, while these radio technologies were not—so the name stuck! You still can't use them illegally, of course; for example, the FCC has been known to cite businesses for using FRS (Family Radio Service) for commercial purposes, since that's outside the scope of the service. But for most boaters, there are no real restrictions on these radios other than the purely technical.

Citizens Band

During the 1970s, Citizens Band (CB) radio became all the rage on the American highways. Inevitably, some of this spilled over onto the water, and for a time, CB was a popular alternative to marine VHF.[67]

With no licensing requirements and even fewer restrictions than VHF—there are, for example, no formal restrictions on channel use, no limits on operating from both land and water, and no requirement that conversations be pertinent or brief— there are some advantages to CB. Most U.S. CB uses SSB modulation, and it runs in a frequency band that occasionally can have some real range improvements on VHF.

However, radios aren't much use without other folks listening to them, and CB is largely unmonitored throughout most of the world. In some pockets of the United States, local fishing fleets might still use them, but for the most part, you're not going to find other boaters with CBs on board these days.

By convention (not law, unlike VHF Channel 16), Channel 9 is used for emergency traffic on CBs. Almost no maritime rescue agencies monitor CB, but some civilian groups, such as REACT (Radio Emergency Associated Communication Teams), attempt to provide coverage.

Hailing usually happens on Channel 19, but that's a trucker convention and may not do you much good out on the water.

Power requirements are low and antenna installation is simple —it will, however, require a separate antenna from any of your other radios on board.

That's an obstacle to both casual conversation and navigational and emergency uses, so CB is slowly dying out on the water.

Family Radio Service (FRS)

FRS is a short-range, unlicensed band largely used by tiny portable walky-talkies that have become popular for reasons of price and portability. People carry them backpacking and skiing, and increasingly use them out on the water.

With a range of around a couple miles and no penetrating

---

[67] Both systems were implemented around the same time, and CB radios were cheaper than VHF, making them a serious consideration for many boaters.

power whatsoever, FRS is no replacement for VHF, either. Yet it shares many of the advantages of CB in that there are few restrictions on use, and the operation is very simple. The tiny sets are often used with headsets on board to facilitate crew communication and are a handy way to stay in touch between dinghy or shore party and the main vessel.

New FRS units can be set up with something like direct dialing, using sub-audible tones to "ring" another user's radio to get their attention. They may come with built-in clocks, GPS, weather channel reception, and "private" call capability—not actually private, but respected by other radios with the same capability when you have directly dialed another particular user.

FRS sets also may have headset connectors to allow hands-free operation. They can be set to voice-activated mode—an alternative to PTT (Push To Talk), this feature uses voice activation to tell the radio to transmit whenever you talk so you don't have to mess around with buttons. This combination of features is often used by crews on larger boats to coordinate docking or anchoring operations.

Radar

Radar[68] also uses radio waves, operating in very different frequency ranges, to bounce off remote targets and create a visual display of the surrounding area on a screen. The technology takes advantage of the strengths of radio (range extending to the horizon, able to penetrate fog and darkness) to provide you with situational awareness in situations where you wouldn't otherwise be able to develop it.

---

[68] RAdio Detection And Ranging, RADAR originally... it's become a common name instead of an acronym over years of use.

You don't have to think much about the details of transmission and reception of those radio waves—the innards of modern radar sets take care of almost all the technical aspects. But it's worth recognizing and remembering that radar is radio-based at heart, and has all the advantages and limitations that go with radio-based technologies. The dependencies, importance of antenna location, and other factors that you consider with other radios all hold just as true for radar, even though the display medium is visual and not audio.

PLB VERSUS AIS MOB

If you've stayed awake through our discussion of other types of radios on board, particularly the emergency variety, you probably noticed that the functional aspects of PLBs and AIS MOB devices are pretty similar. You may even be wondering which one is better or if you should even bother with both.

A PLB provides man-portable EPIRB functionality that will send your emergency call and location directly to an INMARSAT satellite from anywhere in the world and put the GMDSS search and rescue system into immediate operation. In fact, PLB signals do not immediately differentiate between a ship and a personal emergency—the same signal is transmitted in either case. Only by looking up the registration details will SAR professionals know they are looking for an individual in the water rather than a whole boat going down (although your boat may very well have gone down also!).

An AIS MOB device, on the other hand, has a strictly local function. Broadcasting on VHF AIS frequencies, the maximum range is perhaps 5-10 miles.[69] An AIS-equipped vessel must be nearby to receive the distress message.

These factors should help you narrow down the most appropriate device for your personal needs—generally, an AIS MOB unit is the better choice if you can be sure that someone will be around with an AIS unit any time you might end up overboard... for instance, if you have a crew and want to ensure they can come find you if you fall off your own boat.

A PLB, on the other hand, is the clear choice for solo sailors far from shore, who can only rely on the GMDSS system for assistance because there may be no other vessels for hundreds of miles.

A PLB can provide a more exact location—providing it is equipped with GPS—but that location is not immediately accessible to local searchers, only to the GMDSS network. Some high-end PLBs include a homing beacon on 121.5 MHz, just like EPIRBs, but that's generally only of use to specially-equipped SAR craft.

The AIS beacon has no mechanism to transmit GPS, but because the signal is received directly on board the search vessel, it can be used to track you with simple radio direction finding (RDF) equipment or techniques.

Both types of units are available with the usual bells and whistles such as:
- Automatic activation upon submersion
- Flashing rescue beacons
- Able to float
- Small enough to comfortably slip into a foulie pocket or clip to a harness

---

[69] Why not 40-50, like a regular VHF? Because the antenna is, by definition, at water level—the horizon appears much closer than to a mast-mounted antenna.

Radio Installation

Okay, let's face it: most of you didn't install your radio system, and most of you probably aren't going to put in a new one by yourself. You don't even want to know what that spaghetti mess of wiring looks like back there. You either just put up with what some prior owner installed, or you pay some marine electronics technician scandalous rates to take care of that grubby business for you.

But we're going to go into the ins and outs of installation here anyway, for two reasons:

1. So you can have at least an informed overview of the process—enough to understand how the pieces fit together, and enough to oversee and make decisions about the installation or repair process even if you are outsourcing all the wire-cutting and splicing to someone else.
2. In order to understand the connections involved in case you ever find yourself having to troubleshoot your radio setup.

But before we get into the sundry details of choosing a radio and getting it installed, let's talk a little bit about *where* you're going to install it.

Because of the general differences in layout between sailboats and powerboats, your options and preferences may vary depending on which type of boat you have.

Sailboats

The nav station, you say, sailor? That's what we figured.

In fact, your sailboat probably came with a radio, and it was probably already at the nav station. The contrasts starkly with powerboats, where the radios are almost always mounted within reaching distance of the helm

A chronic complaint about sailboaters within the boating community is that they rarely seem to respond to radio calls. The location of the radio belowdecks has much to do with that. Some sailors don't even turn their radio on, in contravention of rules mandating that a radio watch be kept aboard vessels so-equipped. If you can't hear it anyway, why bother?

Well, this is one place where the powerboaters have got things right and the sailors have got it wrong: a radio needs to be located where you will use it.

One hand on the wheel, one hand on the mike will keep you on course and in contact

Once upon a time, and still today in the case of SSBs, that place probably *was* the nav station. It's below, sheltered from the elements, where finicky electronics are protected and the shrieking of the wind wouldn't overwhelm primitive microphones. If you had to sit down and fiddle with the settings to get a signal out, the nav station was probably the best place to do it. And unlike powerboats, the helm for most sailboats is out in the open, sure to get soaked in rain or by big waves... not to mention easily accessed by thieves shopping for expensive electronics.

Today, there are fewer excuses for putting your radio out of the way. In fact, nav stations themselves are shrinking and sometimes evaporating in modern sailboat designs. The primary navigation instrument has become the chartplotter. Where is it at? The helm, naturally, where you most need that information.

Radios have become marinized to withstand the elements out there, or at least have started to come with remote microphone stations that are perfectly happy living on your pedestal.

Powerboats

You powerboaters don't get to gloat, though. Powerboats have their own chronic problems with radio installations. Frequently, they are located in places where engine noise overwhelms the sound of either the radio broadcast or your voice as you try to transmit. Poor installations that are not properly RF (radio frequency)-shielded also feature a wealth of interference from engine electrical output. Or maybe you have multiple helm stations, and while the VHF is located in the main cabin, you spend most of your time steering from the flybridge—out of earshot of the radio.

So, whatever kind of boat you own, if you have your radio someplace where you can't, or find it inconvenient to, use while underway, consider relocating it. If that's too much trouble, at least think about making it more audible in places where you are likely to be sitting while sailing. Many sets have an auxiliary output plug. If you have a regular AM/FM or other sound system wired on the boat already, you can plug the VHF/SSB into that to amplify the sound to reach you.

And, of course, many radios today offer the option of remote stations. These may be the best solution since they offer good access to the radio in whatever place you happen to be spending the most time.

RFI (Radio-Frequency Interference)

A remote station isn't going to help you with RFI, however—and you may need to hire a professional to fully insulate your system against it.

RFI is what you get when other electrical components on

board leak RF energy in the spectrum that your radio operates in. It's another consideration regarding where you should install your radio.

On radios that carry voice traffic, RFI will manifest as loud pops or whines or static in your transmissions or calls that you hear. For other radio devices, like radars, you will see interference as blips or ghosts on the screen where no actual objects are at.

For VHF radios, most RFI is transient and unobtrusive. It's an inevitable side effect of designing a receiver system sensitive enough to pick up the microvolt electrical waves propagating through the atmosphere that it will also pick up even trace amounts of electrical noise in the same frequencies that hit it at closer ranges.

The most common source of RFI is your vessel itself. Your engine, electrical system, and other electronic components are all potential causes of RFI. The electrical fields they generate can hit your radio in one of two ways:

- **Over the air (induction)** — To avoid boring you to death, we didn't bother to describe earlier how radio waves were discovered by messing around with electrical discharges or that Marconi's original sets were powered by big, ugly spark-gap transmitters that blasted up to 14,000 volts between a couple of metal points to generate a signal. But, anyway, electricity discharging itself through the air like that does create a signal, so even small switches or your engine firing is creating radio waves that can potentially be picked up by your antenna.
- **Through the wiring (conduction)** — Another route for RF interference to get into your radio system is directly through the wiring... the power wiring going into the radio can conduct the same spurious signals right into the radio through the electrical system. In modern radios, filtering almost always eliminates or greatly reduces this pathway, however.

In either case, you have two installation options to reduce the problem:

- Shielding the radio
- Eliminating the source

Both are somewhat specialized and time-consuming to perform in practice. However, we mention it here so that you have some idea how to troubleshoot and go about getting a professional to help you eliminate chronic and disturbing RFI. Alternators, electric motors, ignition systems (spark plugs), or even static electricity generated by a rotating propeller shaft can be sources of RFI.

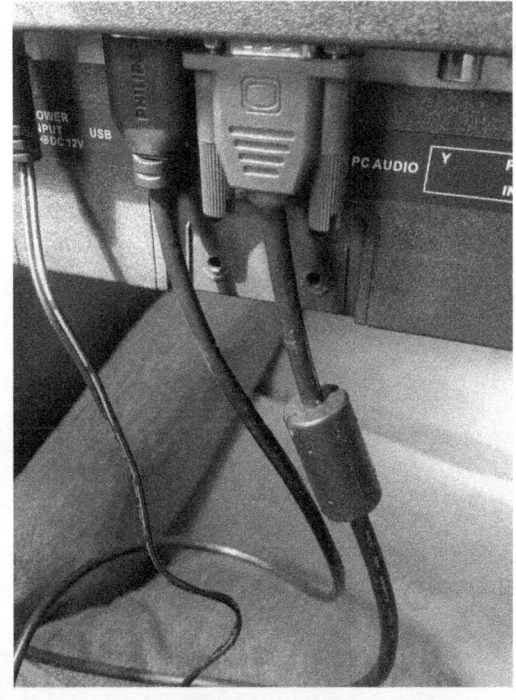

A ferrite on a video display cable can help protect it from radio frequency interference.

Naturally, other radios also generate radio waves that can cause interference. And many boaters actually experience the flip-side of this issue, which is when radio transmissions interfere with other sensitive on-board electrical systems like chartplotters and autopilots. Essentially the same process is required to isolate these systems from spurious interference.

By testing your radio performance systematically in concert with running these systems, you can get a good idea where problems are coming from.

In some cases, the proximity of the radio to the device may be the primary issue. Relocating one or the other (easy in the case of, say, a handheld radio device—not so much if the source is your engine) to a suitably remote location can cure the issue.

Another quick and inexpensive fix can sometimes be had by clamping a ferrite core around the cables leading either to the offending device or the radio. These must be designed appropriately to the frequencies being interfered with, however, so unless you are comfortable tracking down that data, they may be a tool best left to professionals. If you have equipment that has been supplied with a ferrite, however, as many modern marine electronics are, you should be sure that you install the ferrite that comes with the gear as instructed—it will have already been calibrated to the frequencies likely to leak.

VHF Installation and Operation

There are really only three elements to the hardware side of a radio system: a radio, an antenna, and a power source. We'll talk about them as they relate to your VHF system here in the order they are connected.

Power

Marine VHF radios pretty much universally run on 12-volt DC (Direct Current) electricity. Conveniently, this is exactly what is supplied by most recreational vessel DC electrical systems.

This makes wiring a snap. DC systems are two-wire, a positive (+) and a negative (-) wire. By convention, the positive wire is red and the negative is black (on older systems) or yellow (the most recent standard).[70]

Somewhere on the back of your radio, these two wires will go in to provide power. Tracing those wires back will, after some meandering, get to the battery bank.

Those meanderings can be important, however.

At least one of them will likely go through a switch or breaker (usually on your electrical panel) and/or a fuse.

You need to know where these potential troubleshooting points are in the wiring harness before you leave the dock.

The breaker or fuse prevents a short circuit in the radio power

---

[70] According to the American Boat and Yacht Council (ABYC) E-11 electrical standard; since black is also used in AC wiring as a hot wire, the DC negative was switched to yellow to avoid fatal mistakes.

circuit (say, for instance, the wires at the back of the VHF pulled out and crossed one another—instant fire!) by blowing out when the wires are pulling more juice than the radio should ever need. Sometimes, however, this can happen in the course of normal operation.

So, when you flip the radio on and nothing lights up on the front panel, your first troubleshooting steps should be:
- Check the power switch or breaker at the panel
- If the switch is on, check the fuse to see if it is blown
- If those are both okay, check where the wires go into the back of the radio to make sure they are completely connected
- If everything is connected, make sure your primary battery power selector is on and other DC systems are receiving power

A blown fuse is an easy fix, if you know where to look for it... and have a spare on board!

Power problems can go deeper, of course, and this book is not a treatise on solving them. But if you are having performance problems with your radio, power is a good place to start. A transmitter needs juice to make your signal go. Clean connections, delivering full voltage to the radio, can make a world of difference in your signal strength.

The Radio

Although radios have a great many features and options to differentiate them (most of which are covered in the VHF Overview section), they all share some basic features:
- A channel selector and indicator
- Settings for the channel plan
- Volume controls
- Squelch controls

The volume knob often doubles as an on/off switch. That and the channel controls are pretty self-explanatory.

The channel plan setting allows the radio to be set up to conform to U.S., Canadian, or International VHF frequency plans. On a lot of radios, this is not a setting that is easy or obvious to get at, and for good reason—you probably will never need to mess with it.

Squelch

Squelch is a sensitivity setting. It may be a knob or a set of buttons; it tunes the radio to a certain level of noise required to activate the speaker. The setting is strictly to your taste—if you set squelch low, you will hear transmissions of lower power levels, and they may be weak or broken. If you set it high, you will only hear more powerful, clear transmissions... but you may miss calls from further away.

You might set this and forget it, but it's useful to check the setting every once in a while. The level of interference and atmospheric noise is variable, and a setting that is perfect on one day can squelch out completely audible transmissions on the next day. Alternatively, you can keep from getting blasted with static constantly on a noisy day by turning the squelch up.

Hi/Low

Fixed-mount VHF radios have two power levels, 25 watts and 1 watt, usually just labeled HI and LO.

You can switch back and forth, but most people don't pay much attention to this setting. It's something you should be aware of, though, for two reasons.

First, the FCC regulates how much power you can put out on certain channels, and it is illegal, technically, to transmit on high power on these frequencies. Channels 13 and 67 are the ones where you are most likely to notice this restriction, and new radios automatically switch to LOW when you change your selector to these channels, which is one reason most people don't have to worry about it.

Second, it's the courteous and professional thing to do to attempt your calls first on low power to keep from interfering with conversations further away. Reducing your radio call footprint to the minimum necessary range helps preserve the airwaves for everyone. Most of the time, when you're hailing a marina for a slip from just off the breakwater, you don't need to be blasting that conversation 20 miles away at high power.

Other Buttons and Dials

If you take a look at the faceplates of two modern VHFs and count the number of dials and buttons, you might come to the conclusion that the one with more of both is probably the more expensive unit. You might be right, but then again, you might not —like everything else in the modern world, VHF units are becoming primarily software-driven. You are as likely to program your squelch setting through a digital interface as twiddling a knob these days.

This presents you with something of a philosophical choice to make. A radio with a lot of buttons on the front certainly *looks* more complicated, and is, in at least one respect: you have to find the right one at the right time to perform the function you want.

On the other hand, this offers a sort of simplicity: instead of forcing you to go through a multi-level software menu on a tiny display screen, you can quickly and easily access that function with a single button.

The Antenna

As long as the radio is on, the antenna will pick up waves coming in from any station it can see.

When you transmit, the antenna turns the modulated impulses of power into waves that propagate out to the horizon.

The efficiency with which an antenna transmits and receives is measured by its gain, given in decibels (db). Higher numbers equate to more power, as you would expect.

VHF antennas are relatively simple and do not require the fine-tuning of, say, SSB or ham sets.

The total length of the cable run between the radio and the antenna, together with any splices or connections in the cable, will diminish the power going in either direction, just as it would with any other electrical connection. This is not likely to significantly diminish your performance on most vessels, but on large boats with long runs, or in any installation where a lot of splicing has to be done, it's something to consider.

It's almost always best to put the antenna on the uppermost part of your vessel—the top of the tallest mast on sailboats, the highest part of the superstructure on powerboats. The antenna is the part of the system that the line of sight is measured from, so the higher it is, the further your signal will go and the more distant stations you can receive.[71]

The antenna should always be installed as close to vertical as possible. The standard vertical wave antenna doesn't receive or transmit equally at all angles; the most powerful effect is found with signals coming in, or going out, perpendicular to it. Since some masts or structural components are raked, getting the antenna vertical might require an offset. Of course, it will rarely be vertical in practice as you roll and pitch on the waves, but as long as you start off as close as possible, you'll be starting off on the right foot.

VHF antennas can be tiny (look at the average handheld antenna, for example), and on sailboats, with the mast available to get all the height, they often are. This can result in long cable runs, which result in some loss, but the net gain from having the antenna so high is worth it.

Powerboats will usually use large whip antennas, which have higher gain and shorter cable runs but still can't get the height to compare to sailboat antenna mounting.

All that needs to be said about the cable is that it should be of a type and installed in accordance with the radio manufacturer's instructions, and the fewer splices are in it, the better. Signal strength may be lost at each connector.

Handheld VHF Radios

It's a good idea to have a spare for any vital piece of safety equipment on board, and your VHF radio is no exception. Many

---

[71] How high and how far? This isn't that kind of book! But if you want to figure it out for your boat, the formula is:

Range in nautical miles = 2.25 x square root of the height of the antenna in meters

boaters carry one or more handheld VHF units as both a backup for their fixed-mount system and for general utility use. As portable sets, they are easy to use when you can't easily be at the fixed-mount location[72] or to take along when you are out in a dinghy or kayak.

Handhelds have less power and weaker antennas and are necessarily lower than your main antenna, which makes them a distant second in capability to fixed-mount systems. Their maximum transmitting power is only 5 Watts versus the 25 Watts that a fixed-mount system can punch out.

On the other hand, they can receive almost as well, albeit generally at a lesser distance. The quality of reception is more dependent on the transmitting station than the receiver, which is

---

[72] Although if you have a remote microphone station, as discussed above in the Features and Settings section of the VHF Overview, you can do this already.

the same reason your crappy car radio can get your foot tapping to the Rolling Stones a hundred miles away from your favorite FM station.

Modern handheld units are often waterproof and have a similar range of features available at various price points as do fixed-mount radios, including GPS and DSC integration. They usually have rechargeable batteries, and sometimes come with adapters to allow you to use standard disposable battery sizes in a pinch. Chargers often will work off either 12 volt DC or 110 volt AC systems.

One interesting feature available in some waterproof, floating handhelds is a man overboard beacon—when the radio goes in the water, it starts flashing a red LED and automatically goes into Man Overboard distress call mode. Pressing and holding the Distress button sends a DSC Mayday call with the distress type set to Man Overboard and the position included.

If the radio has a detachable antenna, it is possible to boost your transmission quality by attaching it to a regular masthead antenna. The radio transmitting power will not be improved, but your signal will be going out from a higher altitude and a better antenna. Some books suggest your effective output can be increased by around forty percent with this method.[73]

Battery power will fade fast with frequent transmitting.

---

[73] Fletcher, Sue. Reed's VHF/DSC Handbook. Bloomsbury Publishing Plc, 2002.

Glossary

Amidships - The middle of the boat, conventionally as judged between bow and stern; however, may also mean the centerline between both beams.

Aft - At or toward the stern of the boat.

AIS (Automatic Identification System) - An automatic tracking system that broadcasts ship movement and status on VHF channels through short data bursts, which can be received by specialized units and display the ship's location, speed, and heading along with other data.

Ballast - Weight carried on a boat for purposes of increasing stability in the water.

Beam - The measure of the boat's width at the widest portion or the direction relative to that portion.

Berth - (see also Sea Berth, Pilot Berth, V-berth, Quarterberth) An accommodation in which to sleep on board the boat. Some berths may be fixed in place, as with v-berths or bunks, while others may be converted from other components, such as settees or tables which convert into sleeping locations.

Bimini - A canvas awning that can be deployed on a frame to provide protection from sun or weather in the cockpit. May be part of a full-cockpit enclosure (see also Dodger).

Blackwater - Sewage or other waste water from toilets (see also Head).

Bow - The front, or foremost part of the boat.

Bulkhead - A dividing wall between compartments in the boat.

Bung - A stopper, such as a cork or wood plug, used to plug up a hole.

Bridge - The elevated deck on a boat from which it may be steered or commanded. Common to powerboats but unusual on modern sailing vessels.

Cabin - A room inside a boat partitioned off by bulkheads from other interior spaces.

Chainplate - Attachment point from the shrouds to a structural member of the hull on a sailboat.

Cockpit - The well on a boat where the helm station is located. On sailboats, this space is commonly where access to the interior is gained, and is usually furnished with benches and designed for outside entertainment. (see also Bridge).

Deck - Horizontal structure extending the full length of the vessel, providing a place to stand above the cabin, and a roof over the cabin.

Displacement - The weight of the amount of water pushed away when a boat is floating in it. This is also the weight of the boat itself, but displacement is often used as a theoretical measurement discounting current lading.

Dodger - An enclosure around the companionway of a vessel, usually of canvas, with windows to allow forward and side views, designed to provide some protection for crew in the cockpit and prevent heavy seas from sweeping into the companionway hatch.

Draft - The depth of water to which the bottommost portion of the boat extends.

EPIRB (Emergency Position-Indicating RadioBeacon) - An emergency signaling device that transmits on one or more radio frequencies monitored by satellites and aircraft.

Ferrite - A metallic-ceramic cylinder designed to clamp onto an electronics cable to damp down radio frequency interference.

Fiddle - A vertical lip or fixture attached to the edge of a table or counter and designed to prevent items from falling off when the boat is in motion.

Fly-bridge - On a motor vessel, a tall structure over the deck from which the vessel can be controlled. Provides better all-round visibility.

Forward - At or toward the bow of the boat.

Frame - A structural member running athwartship from the keep to the side or side rail of the hull.

Galley - The kitchen or cooking space aboard the boat.

Graywater - Non-sewage waste water, typically from sinks or showers.

Gunwales - Pronounced "gunnel." The vertical projections around the edges of the deck to prevent water getting in or small objects, persons, etc, from falling out on a roll or when the boat is heeled.

Hail - (v.) signaling or calling out to attract attention; the process of formally making initial contact with another station by radio.

Halyard - A line to the top of the mast, used to hoist sails or other flags or equipment.

Head - A marine toilet, or the compartment on board which contains the toilet.

Helm - The steering station on the boat.

HF (High Frequency) - A range of radio frequency electromagnetic waves between 3 and 30 megahertz, with skip properties making them ideal for long range communications.

Holding Tank - A container on board designed to hold waste water until it can be safely and legally disposed of. Commonly for blackwater but increasingly used for graywater holding in some areas.

Hull - The main body of the vessel, containing the cabin and engineering spaces.

Hull Number (HIN) - A standardized serial number, issued by the manufacturer and required in the United States on all vessels manufactured after 1972. The HIN is embossed in the hull on the upper starboard portion of the transom.

ITU (International Telecommunication Union) - A specialized agency of the United Nations responsible for coordinating shared spectrum considerations globally, including allocation of radio spectrum and communications protocols.

Keel - The lowest and principle structural member on the bottom of the vessel. On sailboats, often weighted and pronounced, as a fin or bulb; in such cases, the keel typically refers to the entire structure rather than simply the lowest member.

Lazarette - A small compartment at or near the stern of the vessel, commonly housing the steering gear but frequently used for the storage of equipment or mechanical gear.

Length - The longitudinal measurement from bow to stern at the longest point of the boat.

On Deck - Length on Deck (LOD) refers to the length of the vessel on the main deck from bow to stern. Does not include overhangs such as rails, anchors, or sprits.

Overall - Theoretically, Length Overall (LOA) measures the length of the vessel including fixtures fore and aft of the deck, such as bowsprits, davits, and so forth. Sometimes this measurement is made discounting anchors or other equipment overhanging permanent fixtures. In such cases, the total, complete length of the vessel including both temporary and permanent extensions may be referred to as the Extreme Length of Vessel (ELOV) when that figure is required.

Waterline - The Waterline Length (LWL) measures the length of the vessel at the point where it sits in the water at the designed displacement.

Locker - A compartment accessible from inside or outside the boat in which equipment may be stowed.

'Midships - See "Amidships"

Macerator - A mechanical device which may be used in marine heads to chop up waste before transferring it to a holding tank or disposing of it overboard; helps prevent clogs in the sewage system.

Mast - A vertical spar, usually used to carry sails on sailboats, but often also present on powerboats and used as a platform for antennas, lights, and tackle for hoisting gear or tenders on board.

MF (Medium Frequency) - A range of radio frequency electromagnetic waves between 300 kilohertz and 3 megahertz.

Mooring - 1. A fixed anchoring point in a harbor where a vessel can be secured without deploying her own anchors. Usually marked by a buoy. 2. Commonly used to describe the act of securing a vessel in any location, whether at a mooring or at a dock or pier.

Navigation Desk - Or "Nav Desk" or "Nav Station," a flat or inclined table on the boat designed to provide a position at which charts may be spread out and calculations made for navigating the vessel. Frequently also the location where electronics and the main electrical panel for the boat are located.

Overhead - The ceiling of a cabin, or the top surface in any enclosed compartment on the boat.

PLB (Personal Locator Beacon) - An emergency signaling device that transmits on a frequency monitored by global satellite coverage; designed for individual use, a smaller and less powerful EPIRB device.

Pilot Berth - A bunk typically set into the sides of the main cabin on sailboats. Frequently used as shelf or storage space.

Port - 1. The left-hand side of the boat when viewed aft to fore. Also "Larboard" in older use. 2. A harbor in which ships may be moored or serviced.

Pro word or Procedure Word - Key words with a previously agreed-upon meaning that are used in radio and other communications for clarity. Often chosen for their distinctiveness and sound quality over radio.

Quarter - 1. The two after parts of the ship to either side of the centerline; hence "port quarter" and "starboard quarter." 2. The direction given on the approximate bearing away from the boat along the same lines.

Quarterberth - A berth usually oriented fore and aft and located in either quarter. Typically smaller than a v-berth but often a better sea-berth. Due to the location below and beside the cockpit in many designs, the overhead is usually low and access is restricted, leaving many liveaboards to relegate quarterberths to a storage, rather than sleeping, role.

Restricted Radiotelephone Operator's Permit (RROP) - An FCC (Federal Communications Commission)-issued license that may be obtained by individuals to allow them to legally operate a licensed Ship Station radio internationally or in the HF SSB range.

Rig - (n.)The arrangement and characteristics of masts and sails on a sailing vessel.

RFI (Radio Frequency Interference) - Electromagnetic disturbance generated by electrical impulses that affect electrical circuits and therefore radio reception.

Salon - Or "Saloon." The main cabin in the boat, used for eating or entertaining. In many small boats, the only cabin apart from the head.

SART (Search And Rescue Transponder) - A semi-active transceiver that listens for radar wave signals and broadcasts a response when one is received, indicating the direction and rough distance the SART is from the original radar set. Used for homing in on vessels or individuals in distress.

Seacock - A valve designed to close off thru-hull openings from the interior of the vessel.

Sea Berth - A berth specially designed to secure the occupant while the boat is in motion. Typically equipped with lee cloths, rectangular panels of fabric which are secured at the corners to provide a soft surface for the sleeper to roll against when the vessel rolls or lurches.

Sea-Kindly - An ephemeral characteristic possessed by a vessel related to its ability to ride through rough water in a manner that puts passengers at their ease. A gentle motion combined with adequate performance in heavy seas.

Settee - A long, upholstered or cushioned seat accommodating multiple people. In many small boats, settees represent the main seating in the salon as well as convertible berths.

Ship Station License - An FCC (Federal Communications Commission) license issued to a vessel to permit radio usage internationally, or using an SSB radio.

Shroud - A component of the rigging of a sailboat helping to stay the mast laterally.

SSB (Single-sideband) - A type of modulation used to inject a signal into a radio wave through amplitude modulation in a technique that reduces bandwidth spectrum requirements while maintaining signal

Sole - The floor of the cabin.

Spar - A stout pole of some sort; generically describes masts, yards, gaffs, booms and other various appendages of the boat.

Squelch - A circuit that suppresses the output to the speaker in a radio receiver when the incoming signal falls below a certain threshold; since all radio frequencies have a constant low-level of atmospheric noise and other signal on them, a squelch feature allows only strong, understandable incoming signals to be made audible on the radio set.

Starboard - The right-hand side of the boat when viewed aft to fore.

Stay - A component of the rigging of the sailboat helping to stay the mast fore and aft.

Stem - The foremost structural member at the bow of the vessel.

Stern - The back-most part of the vessel.

Stow - The act of stowing, or putting away, items or equipment.

Stowage - The space or manner of stowing something.

Stringer - A structural member running fore and aft, parallel to the keel.

Transom - The surface forming the stern of the vessel.

Thru-hull - A hole penetrating through the hull of the boat; thru-hulls below the waterline are often controlled with valves (called seacocks) to allow them to be closed.

VHF (Very High Frequency) - A range of radio frequency electromagnetic waves between 30 and 300 megahertz, used for many intermediate range communications signals.

V-berth - A roughly triangular shaped berth, typically in the bows, which often represents the largest and "master" accommodations on board small boats. The unusual shape can make the accommodation difficult to make up.

Well-found - Properly equipped and maintained for the purpose at hand.

More Books For Lubbers

For more information about marine radio use, including personal stories, updates, and the free SSB supplement, see our website at http://marineradio.forlubbers.com!

Need a little more nautical knowledge? Check out...
Lubber's Guides

Because everybody is a lubber sometimes...

Our nautical guidebooks cover the topics that others just assume you already understand. We use fun, plain language to explain the basics of elementary boat-buying, boat-handling, and boat-keeping skills that every mariner and boat owner needs to know.

If you're interested in other fun, easy-to-understand explanations on a variety of nautical subjects, check out http://forlubbers.com to check out our other books!

Of special interest to prospective boat buyers:

The Ultimate Guide to Buying a Boat
Everything you need to know about buying the boat of your dreams without sinking your bank account!

Lazarette - Boomkin - Chine

What are these three words? Well, don't worry about them right now, all right? We'll let you know what to do with them later... keep an eye on our website or follow us on Twitter!

Appendix: VHF Frequency Plans

International, U.S., and Canadian marine VHF channel allocations and their U.S. FCC-designated uses.

New Channel Number	Old Channel Number	Ship Transmit MHz	Ship Receive MHz	Use
1001	01A	156.050	156.050	Port Operations and Commercial, VTS. Available only in New Orleans / Lower Mississippi area.
1005	05A	156.250	156.250	Port Operations or VTS in the Houston, New Orleans and Seattle areas.
06	06	156.300	156.300	Intership Safety
1007	07A	156.350	156.350	Commercial. VDSMS
08	08	156.400	156.400	Commercial (Intership only). VDSMS
09	09	156.450	156.450	Boater Calling. Commercial and Non-Commercial. VDSMS

10	10	156.500	156.500	Commercial. VDSMS
11	11	156.550	156.550	Commercial. VTS in selected areas. VDSMS
12	12	156.600	156.600	Port Operations. VTS in selected areas.
13	13	156.650	156.650	Intership Navigation Safety (Bridge-to-bridge). Ships >20m length maintain a listening watch on this channel in US waters.
14	14	156.700	156.700	Port Operations. VTS in selected areas.
15	15	--	156.750	Environmental (Receive only). Used by Class C EPIRBs.

16	16	156.800	156.800	International Distress, Safety and Calling. Ships required to carry radio, USCG, and most coast stations maintain a listening watch on this channel. See our Watchkeeping Regulations page.
17	17	156.850	156.850	State & local govt maritime control
1018	18A	156.900	156.900	Commercial. VDSMS
1019	19A	156.950	156.950	Commercial. VDSMS
20	20	157.000	161.600	Port Operations (duplex)
1020	20A	157.000	157.000	Port Operations
1021	21A	157.050	157.050	U.S. Coast Guard only
1022	22A	157.100	157.100	Coast Guard Liaison and Maritime Safety Information Broadcasts. Broadcasts announced on channel 16.

1023	23A	157.150	157.150	U.S. Coast Guard only
24	24	157.200	161.800	Public Correspondence (Marine Operator). VDSMS
25	25	157.250	161.850	Public Correspondence (Marine Operator). VDSMS
26	26	157.300	161.900	Public Correspondence (Marine Operator). VDSMS
27	27	157.350	161.950	Public Correspondence (Marine Operator). VDSMS
28	28	157.400	162.000	Public Correspondence (Marine Operator). VDSMS
1063	63A	156.175	156.175	Port Operations and Commercial, VTS. Available only in New Orleans / Lower Mississippi area.
1065	65A	156.275	156.275	Port Operations
1066	66A	156.325	156.325	Port Operations

67	67	156.375	156.375	Commercial. Used for Bridge-to-bridge communications in lower Mississippi River. Intership only.
68	68	156.425	156.425	Non-Commercial. VDSMS
69	69	156.475	156.475	Non-Commercial. VDSMS
70	70	156.525	156.525	Digital Selective Calling (voice communications not allowed)
71	71	156.575	156.575	Non-Commercial. VDSMS
72	72	156.625	156.625	Non-Commercial (Intership only). VDSMS
73	73	156.675	156.675	Port Operations
74	74	156.725	156.725	Port Operations
77	77	156.875	156.875	Port Operations (Intership only)
1078	78A	156.925	156.925	Non-Commercial. VDSMS
1079	79A	156.975	156.975	Commercial. Non-Commercial in Great Lakes only. VDSMS

1080	80A	157.025	157.025	Commercial. Non-Commercial in Great Lakes only. VDSMS
1081	81A	157.075	157.075	U.S. Government only - Environmental protection operations.
1082	82A	157.125	157.125	U.S. Government only
1083	83A	157.175	157.175	U.S. Coast Guard only
84	84	157.225	161.825	Public Correspondence (Marine Operator). VDSMS
85	85	157.275	161.875	Public Correspondence (Marine Operator). VDSMS
86	86	157.325	161.925	Public Correspondence (Marine Operator). VDSMS
87	87	157.375	157.375	Public Correspondence (Marine Operator). VDSMS

88	88	157.425	157.425	Commercial, Intership only. VDSMS
AIS 1	AIS 1	161.975	161.975	Automatic Identification System (AIS)
AIS 2	AIS 2	162.025	162.025	Automatic Identification System (AIS)

Reprinted from the United States Coast Guard website (https://www.navcen.uscg.gov/?pageName=mtVhf)

Appendix: Decoding MMSI Numbers

An MMSI (Maritime Mobile Service Identity) number is always nine digits and has the format of:

MID XXXXXX

...where X represents a number.

MID (Maritime Identification Digits) also represents a number: the country code for the issuing nation. There are too many to list all of them here, but those you are most likely to run across in U.S. waters include:

United States	338, 366, 367, 368, 369
Canada	318
Mexico	345
British Virgin Islands	378
United States Virgin Islands	379
Bahamas	308, 309, 311
Antigua and Barbuda	304, 305
Aruba	307
Bermuda	310

You'll notice all those country codes start with the number 3... that's not a coincidence, either. In general, the first digit of the MID indicates a particular function or region:

0	Ship group, coast station, or station group
1	Search and Rescue aircraft
2	Europe
3	North and Central America and Caribbean
4	Asia
5	Oceania
6	Africa
7	South America
8	Handheld transceiver
9	Other, including EPIRB, AIS, or SART

MMSI can also be used to call groups, with more than one related station being identified (and called) by the group number. This is done by adding digits ahead of the MID. Group identities are prefixed with either 0 (for ship groups) or 00 (for coast station groups). The group number will not necessarily have any relationship to any member station's individual number... for example, all U.S. Coast Guard coastal stations have the MMSI 003669999.

A station can also belong to more than one group.

Several other prefixes have been authorized, sometimes only for a particular country code. In the United States, these include:

Prefix	Use
111	Aircraft; currently only issued to USCG aircraft.
99	Aids To Navigation - Not yet widely deployed but USCG has been testing AIS-visible aids. Consult your LNTMs for details.
98	Launches or other craft associated with a parent ship —the base MMSI will be that of the parent vessel.
970	SART beacon.
972	MOB beacon.
974	EPIRB transmitter. The user identity combines a manufacturer code with a sequence number and does not relate to the vessel the EPIRB is registered with.

A Coast Guard Sector might have a number of stations under the same group number so that a call could be received by any of them.

In case you need them, here are the USCG sector numbers:

Astoria	003669910
Baltimore	003669961
Boston	003669901

Charleston	003669907
Corpus Christi	003669916
Delaware Bay	003669905
Detroit	003669930
Hampton Roads	003669922
Houston/Galveston	003669915
Humboldt Bay	003669909
Jacksonville	003669962
Key West	003669918
Long Island	003669931
Los Angeles/Long Beach	003669912
Miami	003669919
Mobile	003669914
New Orleans	003669908
New York	003669929
North Bend	003669911
North Carolina	003669906
Northern New England	003669921
Port Angeles	003669904
Portland	003669937
San Diego	003669913
San Francisco	003669926
Seattle	003669938

Southeastern New England	003669928
St. Petersburg	003669917
All USCG coast stations	003669999

There are a number of oddities you may run across as MMSI is still evolving; AIS-SART transmitters, for example, have a slightly different code based on the manufacturer rather than the country.

Appendix: GMDSS Explained

The Global Maritime Distress and Safety System is an effort by the IMO to standardize and improve the marine radio safety net. It clarifies certain procedures, equipment standards, and carriage requirements for large and commercial vessels.

You can think of this as an ongoing evolution of the international system of search and rescue conventions that began in the wake of the *Republic* incident and has continued to grow through experience and improving technology. And, just as has always been the case, those high-level developments eventually trickle down to, and improve, the safety of recreational mariners. GMDSS is where the global Digital Selective Calling standards come from, for example, and determines the format and allocation of MMSI numbers.

Although recreational vessels don't have to know anything in particular about GMDSS and don't have to comply with the provisions it makes, it can be useful to understand a little bit about how it is used to organize the global communication and rescue systems. Following GMDSS standards is also a good way to ensure you are in the best possible position to receive assistance through the established SAR channels if you should happen to need it.

The system makes use of both ship-to-shore and ship-to-satellite radio systems and defines a number of other communication protocols such as:

- Telex
- Navtex
- EPIRB and SART[74]

None of these technologies were invented by or for GMDSS, but the system provides a framework for using them together to improve the safety of ocean voyages generally and to improve

---

[74] AIS is not technically a GMDSS technology at time of writing, but modernization efforts are likely to soon incorporate it into this list.

and integrate the global distress monitoring and response network.

GMDSS Areas

IMO started by splitting up the globe into four types of areas, based on the likely requirements necessary for radio distress calling — usually a function of their distance from civilization:

- **A1** - Any area within VHF radio range of a Coast Guard station equipped with DSC reception equipment. This is generally a 20 mile strip around populated coastal areas.
- **A2** - Any areas within MF range of a Coast Guard station equipped with DSC reception equipment, excluding areas meeting the A1 classification. This typically stretches from 20 to 70 miles outside of A1 areas.
- **A3** - The area outside of A1/A2 that is covered by Inmarsat constellation reception. This is essentially the entire globe between 70° North and 70° South.
- **A4** - The region of no hope, lying outside all other areas… the very high latitudes up to the poles

These areas roughly correspond to the recommended equipment for vessels to carry.

Equipment	A1	A2	A3	A4
VHF	✓	✓	✓	✓
SSB	✓	✓	✓	✓
EPIRB			✓	✓
Sat phone				✓
Navtex		✓	✓	✓

SART				✓

GMDSS Capabilities

DSC is an integral component of GMDSS but many recreational mariners will be surprised to learn that their DSC radios are not actually fully compliant with GMDSS services. There are three classes of DSC controller and the radios usually sold to the recreational market are Class D, which lack several features required of commercial units, such as:
- Ability to acknowledge distress calls via DSC
- Automated position polling
- Optional means of cancelling distress alerts
- Automatic service calls

These aren't necessarily important features but they help explain why a Class A set can cost nearly $2,000 while a run-of-the-mill Class D can be had for $300.

Class D incorporates the following capabilities:
- Distress call
- All-ships call
- Individual station call
- Use of distress, urgency, safety and routine priorities
- Nature of distress
- Distress coordinates
- Time for last (distress) position update
- Type of subsequent communications
- Radio VHF channel
- Display
- Receive distress relay and distress acknowledgment calls
- Alarm
- Distress acknowledgement (receive)
- Geographical area call (receive)
- Test call
- Test acknowledgement

At some point—not necessarily very soon—it's likely that the

IMO will do away with general watchkeeping on guard frequencies for most vessels. The ability to call another station will rely on DSC direct calling.

Which is an excellent reason for you to get familiar with DSC as soon as possible.

GMDSS Considerations

Vessels required to comply with GMDSS standards have to meet a number of other specifications in addition to their equipment carriage and capability. Again, as a recreational mariner, you aren't held to these standards... yet it can be useful to see what the rules mandate for larger vessels, since you may want to consider how the logic behind them impacts your own safety considerations.

Satellite Communication

At publication date, INMARSAT is the only satellite communications network that is a provider of GMDSS services.[75] That's because INMARSAT fully implements the distress calling, position-finding, and warning reception that GMDSS calls for. Since the authorities are using those channels for things like ice alerts and radio navigation warnings, you should consider your provider when equipping your vessel with satellite communication services.

Power Supply

GMDSS also specifies triple redundancy for equipment power supplies:
- Normal generator/alternator
- Emergency backup generator/alternator
- Dedicated backup battery

Again, you won't go to the same lengths as a major commercial vessel to comply with these policies, but you should

---

[75] Both Iridium and Thuraya are either in the process of or have indicated the intention to provide GMDSS services.

at least consider ways in which you could make your own power supplies redundant.

Licensing

GMDSS comes with various operator and installer licensing requirements... one of which is the RROP noted in Licensing. Although there are only certain scenarios in which that regulation applies to recreational mariners, some form of training and validation may not be a bad idea for you in any event. United States Power Squadrons are among the more available and reputable trainers for radio users in the United States.

Appendix: Frequency Allocation

Here's a brief overview of the names for all these frequencies, how they fit together, and who is responsible for administering the radio spectrum.

Frequency	Wavelength	Designation	Abbreviation
3–30 Hz	105–104 km	Extremely low frequency	ELF
30–300 Hz	104–103 km	Super low frequency	SLF
300–3000 Hz	103–100 km	Ultra low frequency	ULF
3–30 kHz	100–10 km	Very low frequency	VLF
30–300 kHz	10–1 km	Low frequency	LF
300 kHz – 3 MHz	1 km – 100 m	Medium frequency	MF
3–30 MHz	100–10 m	High frequency	HF
30–300 MHz	10–1 m	Very high frequency	VHF
300 MHz – 3 GHz	1 m – 10 cm	Ultra high frequency	UHF
3–30 GHz	10–1 cm	Super high frequency	SHF

30–300 GHz	1 cm – 1 mm	Extremely high frequency	EHF
300 GHz – 3 THz	1 mm – 0.1 mm	Tremendously high frequency	THF

Agencies Responsible For Setting Frequency Standards

These numbers and ranges are set by the International Telecommunications Union (ITU), now a part of the United Nations. But the agency was originally created in 1865, as the International *Telegraph* Union, with a similar charter to the one it holds today: to set standards and assist in coordinating the use of shared resources to facilitate international communication. Without the ITU to referee international standards, you wouldn't be able to talk to Canadians on a U.S. radio or vice versa.

The ITU has no enforcement power. Treaties and other agreements delegate national agencies to handle the details of spectrum allocation. In the United States, this is handled by the Federal Communication Commission (FCC). In Canada, it is Industry Canada (IC).

While the ITU sets out a block of frequencies for marine use, for example, it is up to the FCC to divide them into the channels and uses that we have described throughout this book. Those are further impacted by coordination with the Coast Guard, and by other, separate international agreements such as the SOLAS treaty, which sets some standards for frequency use.

Appendix: Basic Scripts

These scripts should be considered examples to base your own on. They represent common starting points for conversations you either plan to have regularly, or those you hopefully will never have, but have to get right on the first try!

You can write out or type up your own, with your own vessel's name and particulars, and post them near your radio for easy reference.

These conversations can be conducted on various channels, as described in the text, depending on the context, so any channel transitions that might occur are not described (with one exception). In most cases, these are short enough that they would be primarily conducted without switching.

We've had to imagine some scenarios, naturally. For the most part, information that you will be expected to fill in on the fly will be indicated in parentheses, italics and underlined, for example: *(your vessel's name x3)*.

Mayday

Mayday, Mayday, Mayday, this is (your vessel's name x3) Mayday

Our position is (give your current position)

(State the nature of the emergency)

(Say what kind of help you need)

We have (number of people on board) people on board.

(Give a description of your boat)

Over

Start a Conversation

(Target vessel's name x3), this is (your vessel's name x3), over.

(Your vessel's name,) this is (target vessel's name) go ahead.

(Target vessel's name), let's go up the channel six-eight, channel six-eight, over.

(Your vessel's name,) roger that, going up to channel six-eight.

Securité

Securité, Securité, Securité, this is (your vessel's name x3).

(Your vessel's name) is a (your vessel's description, usually including length) (give a description of your situation or intentions, e.g. "Heading northbound through Dodd Narrows").

Any concerned traffic can contact (Your vessel's name) on (whatever channel you plan to monitor, usually 16),

Making Passing Arrangements (How do I Call a Freighter?)

(Target vessel's name x3), this is (your vessel's name x3), over.

(Your vessel's name,) this is (target vessel's name) go ahead.

(Target vessel's name), we are the (your vessel description) off your (describe your relative position to them, e.g. "Astern of you."). We are planning to pass you on your (port/starboard) side if that works for you, over.

Roger, (Your vessel's name), understand you intend to pass us on our (port/starboard) side, we'll hold our current course and slow down a little to let you by.

Copy that, (Target vessel's name), much appreciated. This is (Your vessel's name), out.

Verifying Intentions

(Target vessel's name x3), this is *(your vessel's name x3),* over.

(Your vessel's name,) this is *(target vessel's name)* go ahead.

(Target vessel's name), we are the *(your vessel description)* northbound in the fairway bound for the fuel dock. Looks like you may be backing out into the channel ahead of us, just wanted to see what your intentions were, over.

Uh, roger, we're a little hung up here at the moment, _(Your vessel's name)_, we'll wait until you pass before we pull out, over.

Thank you, we'll move right on by. _(Your vessel's name),_ out.

Calling a Marina To Arrange a Slip

Marinas often monitor frequencies other than the normal hailing channels. This is often a regionally agreed-upon channel or sometimes just one they've picked randomly, but check local resources or guidebooks before calling them, lest your plaintive calls eventually receive a reply from some annoyed local that "Maple Bay Marina isn't on 16, switch to 66 Alpha."

Maple Bay Marina, Maple Bay Marina, Maple Bay Marina, this is _(your vessel's name x3)_, over.

Maple Bay Marina replies
Hello, Maple Bay, we are a _(your vessel length overall) (sail or power)_-boat looking for moorage for _(number of nights)_, over.

Be ready to respond to questions about your preferred side to tie up on and dimensions such as your beam and draft. You might also want to inquire about power at the slip, since different shore power plugs may be available. For example:

(Your vessel's name), will you need an electrical connection, and do you prefer port or starboard side tie?

We do need 30-amp power connection and prefer a bow-in, starboard side tie, if that's available, Maple Bay.

Bibliography

Adamson, Lee, and Natasha Brown. "Shipping Emergencies - Search and Rescue and the GMDSS." Focus on IMO. March 1999.

Binns, John "Jack" Robinson, and Virginia Utermohlen Lovelance. "Dots and Dashes: Adventures at the Dawn of the Wireless Age." Unpublished manuscript, 2018.

"Easy Solutions to Radio Frequency Interference." Accessed February 24, 2020. http://www.dieselduck.info/machine/03%20electricity/radio_interference.htm.

Federal Communications Commission. "Enforcement Bureau Reminds Boaters of Marine Radio Rules." United States Government, May 31, 2011. http://transition.fcc.gov/eb/Public_Notices/DA-11-970A1.html.

Fletcher, Sue. Reed's VHF/DSC Handbook. Bloomsbury Publishing Plc, 2002.

FRGS. AFRIN, George Meegan. "Shipboard English for Japanese Pilots." Review of Graduate School of Maritime Sciences, Kobe University, no. 5 (July 2008): 1–25.

Glidden, William C. "The Coast Guard's VHF-FM National Distress System: Analysis for Recapitalization." Thesis, Naval Postgraduate School, 1991.

Harris, Mike. Communications at Sea. Dobbs Ferry, NY: Sheridan House, 2003.

IMO. "International Convention for the Safety of Life at Sea (SOLAS)." London 1 November 1974. UN Treaty Series Vol. 1184 p. 278, 1974.

IMO Sub-Committee on Safety of Navigation, and Rijeka College of Maritime Studies. "IMO Standard Marine Communication Phrases." International Maritime Organization. April 4, 2000, NAV46/INF.4 edition, sec. Agenda Item 9.

Maloney, Elbert S. Communications Afloat. 1st U.S. ed. Chapman's Nautical Guides. New York: Hearst Marine Books,

1991.

Mercz, László. Marine VHF Radio Handbook. 1st ed. Versoix: Mercator Pub, 2010.

National Imagery and Mapping Agency. "International Code of Signals For Visual, Sound, and Radio Communications." International Code of Signals. Bethesda, Maryland: United States Government, 2003. http://www.seasources.net/PDF/PUB102.pdf.

Protheroe, Ernest. Every Boy's Book of Railways and Steamships. The Religious Tract Society, 1911.

"Radio Regulations." International Telecommunications Union, 2016.

Ricker, Harry. "Troubleshooting Your Radio Equipment." ARRL Newsletter, November 1993.

"Ship Radio Stations | Federal Communications Commission." Accessed February 24, 2020. https://www.fcc.gov/ship-radio-stations.

Steinberg, Eric. "SSB/HF Radio Applications in Modern Sailing Vessels." Farallon Electronics, 2003. https://pacificcup.org/kb/ssbhf-radio-applications-modern-sailing-vessels.

United States Coast Guard. "EMERGENCY RADIO PROCEDURES," 2019.

———. "Guidance for 'Good Samaritan' Vessels Assisting in Maritime Search and Rescue." U.S. Coast Guard Rescue Coordination Center Juneau, 2018.

U.S. Coast Guard. "Radio Watchkeeping Regulations." Accessed February 24, 2020. https://www.navcen.uscg.gov/?pageName=mtWatch.

U.S. Marine Corps. Radio Operator's Handbook. 3rd-40.3B ed. Field Manuals. United States Government, 2001.

Weil, David. "Rescue Requirements Spelled Out." The Log, February 8, 2006. https://www.thelog.com/ask-the-attorney/rescue-requirements-spelled-out/.

(N.d.).

www.ingramcontent.com/pod-product-compliance
Lightning Source LLC
Chambersburg PA
CBHW022114040426
42450CB00006B/689